The Birmingham Six and other cases

To Francis Bennion,
whose expression of sympathy
deserve nothing less than
the author's profound gratitude.

Louis
1.xii.1998

The Birmingham Six
and other cases

Victims of Circumstance

Louis Blom-Cooper

Duckworth

First published in 1997 by
Gerald Duckworth & Co. Ltd.
The Old Piano Factory
48 Hoxton Square, London N1 6PB
Tel: 0171 729 5986
Fax: 0171 729 0015

A catalogue record for this book is available
from the British Library

ISBN 0 7156 2813 5

Typeset by Ray Davies
Printed in Great Britain by
Redwood Books Ltd, Trowbridge

Contents

Prologue

This short book is about the 'miscarriages of justice' which have disfigured the scene of criminal justice in recent years. It explores the public misconception about, and the professional failure to explain the function of, the Court of Appeal. To that end the book deploys the crop of recent cases to illustrate the specific issues in the criminal process – the true value of circumstantial evidence, the exclusivity of the jury's role as the decision-maker in determining an accused's guilt or innocence, the provisions in successive Acts of Parliament which have prescribed the powers of the Court of Appeal, and the problems posed for the future of criminal justice.

To unravel the intricacies of the trial and appellate process, the book relies heavily on the case of the Birmingham Six as a prime producer of the undoubted confusion of thought, both among informed commentators as well as untutored citizens, that exemplifies the current loss of public confidence in the system.

The six men who were convicted at Lancaster Crown Court in August 1975 of the terrorist murder of twenty-one people in two public houses in the centre of Birmingham on 21 November 1974, walked free from their imprisonment in March 1991 as a result of a successful, third attempt to have the jury's verdict set aside. The immediate public response to the quashing of the convictions was that they had been the victims of a 'regrettable miscarriage of justice'. That was the precise phrase applied to the case of the Birmingham Six and other notorious criminal cases of that period, by no less a judicial figure than the Master of the Rolls, Lord Woolf of Barnes, on the occasion of his address at the Service of Thanksgiving in St Paul's Cathedral for the life of Lord Taylor of Gosforth, the Lord Chief Justice of England from 1992 to 1996, who died on 28 April 1997.

At the same time the Home Secretary, in the course of correspondence with the Birmingham Six over the level of the compensation offered, expressed his apologies for the miscarriage of justice they had suffered. And the distinguished writer and columnist in the *Independent*, Polly Toynbee, wrote, in welcoming Chris Mullin MP as the new chairman of the Home Affairs Select Committee, that 'with very little support, in the face of scathing indifference from many in his own party, he ploughed a lonely furrow *in proving the innocence* of the Birmingham Six' (italics supplied).[1]

A miscarriage of justice equals, in the public's mind, innocence of the crime. Only in one sense can it be said that justice (or, more accurately, the process of criminal justice) miscarries in its final result, in that the verdict of the trial court, for a variety of reasons, cannot be upheld. The conviction becomes wrongful; and if the convicted person is in prison he is set free. That explanation of the criminal process, however, is far too simple. The successful appeal against a guilty verdict by the jury, so the argument runs, restores the accused to the status of an innocent person which he possessed at the beginning of the trial. That is not so. The law is, strictly speaking, unconcerned with guilt or innocence. Its concern is conviction or acquittal. Has the Crown proved its case? The jury's verdict of not guilty is unequivocally and incontestably to maintain the presumption of innocence. It is the end of the affair. The jury is unaccountable for any verdict of acquittal. But a jury's verdict of guilt which is overturned by the Court of Appeal, in law, is only a wrongful conviction. The presumption of innocence which subsists only so long as the accused is unconvicted is not revivified. On conviction it is replaced. The Court of Appeal cannot substitute itself for the jury and re-try the case. That is not its function. It must oversee the fairness of the trial and satisfy itself that there was evidence on which the jury could properly convict. The jury is exclusively the decision-maker.

The Court of Appeal which freed the six men in March 1991 was at pains to say that, in quashing the conviction of August 1975, it was neither obliged nor entitled by the Criminal Appeal Act 1968 'to say whether we think that the appellant is innocent'. To emphasise that the quashing of a wrongful conviction was not mere legal verbiage, the Court added: 'This is a point of great constitutional importance. The task of deciding whether a man is guilty falls on the jury. We are concerned solely with the question whether the verdict of the jury can stand.' The Court concluded that because of (a) the flawed forensic evidence relating to traces of explosive materials on three of the appellants and (b) the inadmissibility of statements made in the course of the police interviews, the convictions had been improperly obtained; the jury's verdict could not stand.

This book seeks to explain the 'point of great constitutional importance'. Like the Court of Appeal, I am in no position to answer the question whether the six men are or are not innocent of the crimes committed on 21 November 1974. That question may remain a matter of speculation. Were the jury not to have taken into account the two matters to which I have just referred, would its verdict have been the same? While no one can properly say that the six men were guilty, it is nevertheless a proper exercise to study and analyse the evidence which was heard by the jury and which has not at any time been discarded or discredited by the Court of Appeal so that the public can supply its own answer to the question. While some will adhere to the opinion that the Six are men who were the victims of outrageous circumstances, others may conclude that the verdict of guilty was a wrongful conviction and, adopting the strict legal position of the Court of Appeal, remain agnostic about whether they were implicated in terrorist crime. The law, as it stood from 1966 until the Criminal Appeal Act 1995, had made a clear distinction between wrongful convictions as a result of some defect in the trial process (which may or may not have affected the quantity or quality of the evidence adduced at trial) and those which flowed from a clear misjudgment of the evidence by the jury or a misdirection by the judge of the law or his evaluation of the evidence which might have distorted the jury's assessment of it.

The Birmingham Six case featured among a crop of cases in the 1970s which finally ended up, a decade or more later, with the convictions being quashed for a variety of reasons emerging from unfair trials. Not all of them were terrorist cases, although some, like the Guildford Four and Judith Ward, did involve terrorist activity in mainland Britain. Other cases stemmed similarly from improperly obtained admissions arising out of police interviews. The most recent example – July 1997 – was the case of the Bridgewater Three who had their convictions quashed for the murder of a boy delivering newspapers at a West Midlands farmhouse. All the cases pre-dated the Police and Criminal Evidence Act 1984 which substantially reformed the process of interviewing suspects held in police custody.

What I have done is to lay before the reader the evidence which was led at the trial of the Birmingham Six in 1975. I have excluded everything else that was said and done about the two matters to which I have referred. What remained of the evidence was all circumstantial. The trial judge told the jurors that if they concluded that the admissions made to police officers were unreliable, there was insufficient other evidence to sustain a guilty verdict. He said that the circumstantial evidence amounted to suspicion, was even highly suspicious. But it could not amount to proof of guilt. The judge added that if the circumstantial evidence stood alone, he would have withdrawn the case from the jury, which was cited verbatim in the judgement of the House of Lords in the subsequent civil action brought unsuccessfully by the six men against the police and the Home Office. Given that the case was, in fact, left to the jury, that was an opinion that the jury could, if it wished, have rejected. On sentencing the six men the judge said: 'You stand convicted on the clearest and most overwhelming evidence I have ever heard.' What then should we make of the residual circumstantial evidence? Could it sensibly maintain a finding of guilt or does it constitute nothing more than deep suspicion?

In assessing the circumstantial evidence, I have looked only at the transcripts of arguments on both sides when the appeals were heard on reference to the Court of Appeal in 1987 and 1991. I have extracted and relied on only those factual matters that were unchallenged, indeed mostly unchallengeable. I have furthermore checked the details against the facts contained in the comprehensive account by Chris Mullin, the Labour MP for Sunderland South, in his book *Error of Judgment: the truth about the Birmingham Bombings* published in 1986, with a revised edition in 1997. I have endeavoured (I hope successfully) to gather together all the uncontroversial facts in a way in which the reader (imagining himself or herself in a daydream as a member of a retrospectively empanelled jury) can draw the appropriate inferences from those facts.

To assist the hypothetical daydreaming juror, I move on to consider other aspects of the criminal justice system. Circumstantial evidence is often (too often) treated as an inferior brand of probative material. In practice it is as good as, if not of better quality than direct testimony produced by fallible eye-witnesses, made the more uncertain in its validity by the recognition that we see and hear with our whole person, and under certain conditions our eyes and ears become instruments which serve our desires, partisanship and biases. Yet there is a persistent denial that circumstantial evidence is often superior in quality to other evidence.

An intriguing, imaginary dialogue between prosecuting and defence counsel in a criminal trial in Scotland on the value of circumstantial evidence appears in a detective novel, *The Dear Old Gentleman* by George Goodchild and C.E. Bechhofer Roberts (who wrote under the *nom de plume* of 'Ephesian' about the life and speeches of F.E. Smith) published by Jarrolds Publishers in 1935:

> then he [the Advocate Depute] spoke of circumstantial evidence, pointing out to us ... that it is a fallacy to suppose that

circumstantial evidence is unreliable. It depends on the kind and nature of circumstantial evidence for very often ... circumstantial evidence is far more satisfactory than what is called direct evidence. It is liable to corruption: a direct witness may lie; he may say he saw what he never he saw; he may dream that he saw what he never saw. But when the evidence consists of isolated little circumstances, none of them pointing directly to the deed, none of them constituting a deed directly, but all requiring to be placed together and woven together with other circumstances, and when all of these form one consistent chain, linking one thing with another and one person with another, that is most satisfactory evidence ....

If it is completely done, if the circumstances are conclusive, if coincidences as to time and place accord, if other elements, unsuspected and unforeseen and impossible to be prepared, are found exactly to accord with the result of a particular fact to which this enquiry is made – this ... is more satisfactory than if you had one or two witnesses saying that they actually saw the crime done

The defence advocate in reply said:

Circumstantial evidence ... was all very well in its way – undoubtedly it had convicted many guilty prisoners who otherwise would have escaped the just penalty of their crimes – but it must be conclusive; it was not enough that it should merely point towards a person; no, it must so encompass him with the absolute certainty of his guilt, it must so exclude any possible alternative solution that there could not be the slightest doubt of any kind in a reasonable jury's mind that he and only he was guilty.

Public perception of criminal trials may have weakened the place of circumstantial evidence as a prime factor in a jury's evaluation of guilt and innocence of an accused. Such perceptions have resulted in large part from numerous instances portrayed by crime fiction, the cinema and television (including even radio). Few of us can fail to remember and recall watching or hearing a fictional account of a case in which the prime suspect is engulfed by circumstantial evidence blazoning his or her palpable guilt, only for the truth to emerge in the shape of the diligent crime investigator or the masterly cross-examination of a surprise witness by defence counsel revealing the real culprit, preferably with an eleventh-hour *tour de force*. Circumstantial evidence has thus become suspect in the public mind as the best or even the most powerful tool towards providing the answer to a criminal event.

Another part of this book considers the powers of the Court of Appeal to allow or dismiss an appeal against conviction. Much of the confusion about miscarriages of justice and wrongful convictions stems from the lack of clarity of language used by Parliament. Language is often a cussedly independent tool of social intercourse and communication. Given the circumstances of contemporary opinion about crime and justice, a metaphor such as miscarriage of justice has become so ingrained in public usage that we are no longer consistently aware of the imagery of the phrase. We tend to misapply it. Miscarriage by a mother of her unborn child is a part of, but a defect in, the natural process of childbirth. Justice is a man-made concept and not part of nature. What, moreover, did the legislature mean to tell the judges by the use of the phrase, 'unsafe or unsatisfactory'? The lexicographers are, not unnaturally, bewildered by the lawyers' handling of the English language.

Finally, there is a section on the mode of trial for serious crime. Trial by jury is the embodiment of the English sense of fairness to accused persons. Guilt should be achieved only as a result of the decision of twelve people who are drawn from among the ordinary population. The professionalism of the legally qualified is not to be entrusted with such a momentous decision for the individual. Is that attitude likely to prevail into the twenty-first century?

Jury trial has always had its proponents, both within and outside the legal profession, as the only sure foundation of an impartial and acceptable system for administering criminal justice in the higher courts. It has also had its detractors. In 1844 the author of the *Comic History of England* said, in words that have a contemporary ring, that it was 'difficult to get the British bosom into a sufficiently tranquil state to discuss this great subject, for every Englishman's heart will begin bounding like a bonce [a marble] at its bare mention'.[2] Fifty years earlier Jeremy Bentham wrote:

> I give it [trial by jury] to those who choose to have it, in cases in which they choose to have it and not unless they insist upon having it: looking upon it as an institution admirable in barbarous times, not fit for enlightened times, necessary as matters stand in England.[3]

In contemporary Britain, the most compelling proponent of trial by jury has been Lord Devlin in his oft-quoted claim that the jury 'is the lamp that shows that freedom lives'.[4] Professor Glanville Williams, a leading academic criminal lawyer who died only recently, was doubtful that, whatever else may be claimed for the jury, our civil liberties have historically been sustained by juries. He wrote in 1955:

> Most of the great pronouncements on constitutional liberty from the eighteenth century onwards have been the work of judges, either sitting in appellate courts or giving directions to juries, and the assumption that political liberty at the present day depends upon the jury is 'merely folk lore'.

The detractors are gaining in number, but must still be regarded as evincing a minority view.

The motivation for this book has been the desire to redress the balance in public perception of the criminal justice system. Some of the traditional confidence in the pre-eminence of English criminal law has been doubted, if not dented, by cases such as that of the Birmingham Six. Restorative justice – a phrase much paraded by reformers of the criminal justice system – is applicable to victims and offenders to whom conciliation and mediation is the preferred option to the infliction of punishment on the offender. But it is an expression that is apt to describe the need to ensure justice to the accused and the public which seeks legitimacy for inflicting punishment on the convicted wrongdoer.

The composition of the book has been, with one exception, a single-handed affair. Charles Blake, a former distinguished lawyer in Government service, provided me with enormous assistance – helping research legal material (some of it recondite and obscure) correcting my mistakes and helping me to overcome my inadequacies in the art of information technology. To be computer illiterate is a real handicap nowadays, but not so serious a handicap as being grammatically incorrect.

I must not sign off the preface without thanking the publishers, Duckworth, for their preparedness to embark upon an outmoded practice of pamphleteering, a respectable vehicle for engaging in propaganda – in this case the promotion of a civilised system of criminal justice.

Notes

1. *Independent*, 31 July 1997, p. 17.
2. Gilbert à Becket, *The Comic Blackstone* (1844), London, 187
3. Draft of a *Code for the organisation of the Judicial Establishment in France* (1970) *Works*, ed. Bowring 1843. IV. London, 324.
4. *Trial by Jury* (1956) Hamlyn lectures, 8th Series, London, 164.

Diary of Events

30 Jan. 1972	'Bloody Sunday': thirteen killed in Londonderry.
24 Mar. 1972	Stormont Parliament and government suspended. Direct rule by Secretary of State, Mr William Whitelaw.
18 April 1972	Widgery report on 'Bloody Sunday' (HL 101, HC 220).
3/4 Feb. 1974	Twelve people killed in a coach on M62 by an exploded bomb. Judith Ward later charged and convicted.
5/6 and 13/14 Nov. 1974	Two separate terrorist attacks on public buildings in Birmingham.
21 Nov. 1974	Bombs planted by the Provisional IRA causing explosions in two public houses in Birmingham killed 21 people and injured 184. Five men arrested at Heysham for the Birmingham bombings. A sixth man was arrested the following day.

29 Nov. 1974	Prevention of Terrorism (Temporary Provisions) Act 1974 passed.
Oct./Nov. 1974	Explosions caused at public houses in Guildford and Woolwich.
Nov./Dec. 1974	76 people arrested. Only Guildford Four prosecuted together with Anne Maguire and six others for related offences.
15 Aug. 1975	Birmingham Six convicted of terrorist murder of 21 people.
30 Mar. 1976	Application by Birmingham Six for leave to appeal refused by Court of Appeal.
15 July 1976	Fourteen prison officers from Winson Green Prison acquitted of assault on the Birmingham Six.
16 Nov. 1977	McIlkenny and others issue a writ against the Chief Constable of the West Midlands and the Home Office claiming damages for assault by police and prison officers.
17 Jan. 1980	The action in *McIlkenny* v *Chief Constable of West Midlands* is struck out by the Court of Appeal.
3 July 1980	The House of Lords grants leave to appeal in the *McIlkenny* case.

19 Nov. 1981	House of Lords dismisses appeal in the *McIlkenny* civil case.
July 1986	First edition of Mullin's *Error of Judgment* published.
28 Jan. 1988	First reference appeal to the Court of Appeal by Birmingham Six dismissed.
17 Mar. 1989	First reference appeal by Bridgewater Three dismissed by Court of Appeal.
July 1990	Interim Report of the May Commission of Inquiry into the case of the Guildford Four (HC 556).
28 June 1990	The Maguire convictions quashed by the Court of Appeal.
27 Mar. 1991	Second reference appeal by the Birmingham Six to the Court of Appeal successful. Royal Commission on Criminal Justice (Runciman Commission) set up.
17 Sept. 1991	Judith Ward's case referred to Court of Appeal, although she had not appealed her 1974 conviction.
4 June 1992	Judith Ward's conviction quashed by Court of Appeal.
July 1993	Runciman Commission reports.

19 July 1995   Criminal Appeal Act 1995 passed, setting up Criminal Cases Review Commission.

Jan. 1997   Revised edition of Mullin's *Error of Judgment* published.

31 Mar. 1997   Criminal Cases Review Commission (CCRC) starts to receive applications for reference to the Court of Appeal and takes over existing cases from Home Office.

3 July 1997   Case of Daniel McNamee referred to the Court of Appeal (first case referred by the CCRC).

31 July 1997   Judgment of Court of Appeal in Bridgewater Three second reference appeal delivered, quashing convictions.

22 Sept. 1997   Case of Mahmood Mattan (hanged for murder in 1954) referred to Court of Appeal by CCRC.

I

Introduction

The Court of Appeal concluded its 168-page judgment in the Birmingham Six case,[1] ten years ago, with the memorable, fated peroration, 'the longer this hearing has gone on, the more convinced this Court has become that the verdict of the jury was correct'. Dr Rosemary Pattenden, in her scholarly book, *English Criminal Appeals, 1844-1994*, described that conclusion as 'the now infamous remark'.[2] Dr Pattenden expressed her surprise at the degree of confidence which the Court displayed in the jury's verdict, on the ground that the main evidence against the Birmingham Six[3] at their trial had been their confessions and the forensic evidence of Dr Skuse, and only '*some circumstantial evidence*' (italics supplied). That view became, and has remained prevalent among many both serious[4] and amateur commentators, but does it reflect a misjudgment of the case, when viewed objectively and without bias? What value do we place on the verdict of the trial court, when the entrails of the unarticulated decision of the jury are picked over in the minutest detail? What do we mean by the verdict being 'unsafe' – or 'unsafe or unsatisfactory', as it was before the change in the Criminal Appeal Act 1995 – in order to set aside the jury's verdict? If one aspect of the case is found to be unsatisfactory, what should we say about what remains valid in the case? And what indeed should we say of the future of trial by jury? These are not idle questions: they go to the heart of a civilised system of criminal justice.

II

The Ingredients of the Crown's Case at Trial

The Birmingham Six were tried at Lancaster Crown Court in the summer of 1975 before Mr Justice Bridge (later Lord Bridge of Harwich) and a jury. (The venue for the trial was moved from Birmingham, both to minimise the possible impact of any local prejudice and to select a suitable court for security: the court and prison in Lancaster are housed in the Castle.) The Six were charged on an indictment containing 24 counts. The first 21 were counts of murder, each of the deceased victims who were killed as a result of the bombing of two public houses in Birmingham on 21 November 1974 being the subject of the separate counts. The 22nd count charged the six men together with three others with having, between August and November 1974, conspired to cause explosions likely to endanger life or to cause damage to property. (The 23rd and 24th counts charged two of the three others with possessing explosives.)

Each of the Six was convicted by the jury on 15 August 1975 on all the 21 counts of murder, and mandatorily sentenced to life imprisonment. The jury had retired to consider its verdict at 3.33 p.m. on 14 August 1975 and delivered its verdict at 12.28 p.m. the following day after 6½ hours' deliberation. It decided unanimously on 132 charges. Mr Justice Bridge specifically made no minimum recommendation under section 1(2) of the Murder (Abolition of Death Penalty) Act 1965: see letter to *The Times* by Mr Justice Bridge of 2 August 1975 in which he explained why he had thought it right not to make a recommendation of a minimum term to be served.[5] The jury was discharged from returning a verdict on the conspiracy count in respect of the Six. At no stage after indictment was the conspiracy charge raised. It remains on the court file, with no verdict recorded. Had the jury acquitted on the murder charges it would have been asked to say whether the evidence amounted to the less onerous proof of an agreement to cause explosions. No mention of the conspiracy charge was made in the appeal courts. One of the other three was acquitted on count 22, but was convicted, on his admission, of possessing explosives. The other two were convicted of both the conspiracy (count 22) and possessing explosives (counts 23 and 24).

On 30 March 1976 the Six applied for leave to appeal against their conviction to the Court of Appeal (Criminal Division), presided over by the Lord Chief Justice, Lord Widgery. No complaint was then made as to the trial judge's ruling on the trial-within-a-trial, that confessions made by the Six were admissible in evidence. All the grounds of appeal were directed at alleged failures of the judge in the conduct of the trial. The applications for leave to appeal were dismissed. There the matter rested until the case was referred back to the Court of Appeal by the Home Secretary, Mr David (now Lord) Waddington, in 1987 and, for a second time, by Mr Kenneth (now Lord) Baker in August 1990 who, on the day of the Court of Appeal's judgment on 27 March 1991, announced the setting up of the Royal Commission on Criminal Justice (the Runciman Commission). Two years later, in July 1993, the Runciman Commission recommended the depoliticising of the reference power in favour of a Criminal Cases Review Authority to consider all alleged miscarriages of justice. The Criminal Cases Review Commission (as it was legislatively described) was duly set up under the Criminal Appeal Act 1995 and began to receive applications after 31 March 1997. Its first reference, in the case of Daniel McNamee, was made in July 1997.

There were three components of the Crown's case against the Six: there was the evidence relating to the admissions made during police interviews in the days following the bombing; there was the scientific evidence that tended to show contemporaneous handling of explosive material by three of the Six – 'the two central chapters in the story', on which the Six primarily founded their appeal[6] – and there was the circumstantial evidence. On the second reference to the Court of Appeal in August 1990 the police interviews with McIlkenny were successfully impugned, which had a domino effect on all the six men's statements. They had all become suspect and thus unreliable. At that stage the scientific evidence was proved to be defective when Dr Skuse's forensic laboratory tests were called into question; in any event the Crown conceded that its case did not need any such bolstering, and there never was any scientific evidence against the three others; against the fourth it was tenuous. Given the deficiencies in the first two components, what weight could be attached to the third? On its own, could it suffice to produce a verdict of guilty? The trial judge (Mr Justice Bridge) told the jurors that if they concluded that the admissions were unreliable, they could not properly bring in a verdict of guilt. Indeed, if the third component had stood alone – the circumstantial evidence – he would have withdrawn the case from the jury. But was he right in that regard? While the advocates of a wrongful conviction could in support justly point to the judge's view, they could not in any way disturb the picture which had been presented to the jury of the totality of the circumstantial evidence. On sentencing the six men the judge said that they had been convicted 'on the clearest and most overwhelming evidence I have ever heard'.

The circumstantial evidence in totality was substantially unchallenged and was free-standing; it was powerful and compelling; and at no time since the trial has it been added to, or detracted from. It is possible, therefore, to re-examine and analyse it intact, uncontaminated by, and dissociated from the context of the other evidence at trial. What are the series of coincidences and circumstances which might show inconsistency with a claim of innocence? What this author has attempted to do is to display the uncontroverted facts and then to postulate reasonable conclusions from that factual material. Since, in the very nature of many criminal events, there is bound to be an absence or deficiency in direct evidence against the perpetrators, there is no vice in accumulating circumstantial facts from which to draw the inescapable inference of criminal responsibility. Indeed, there should be every encouragement to prefer the search for evidence which is not primary. Once established, the circumstances are no more likely to be misinterpreted than direct or primary evidence which calls for inferential judgment.

The trial judge's direction

The validity of the jury's verdict was made easier to understand by the manner of the summing-up. Leaning favourably towards the defence's case, Mr Justice Bridge said:

> It is only right to say that if the case stopped there [meaning the relevant background and circumstantial evidence] and if there was not very much positive evidence on which the Crown could rely, I would not have left this case for your consideration, because if you put upon those matters of background the sinister construction which the Crown invite you to, no matter how far they go, they do not go beyond raising suspicion; strong suspicion perhaps, but these matters, if they do show motive, opportunity and an intention to make a getaway still fall a long way short of anything that anyone could possibly regard as proof, that any one of these six men participated in the planning or the placing of the explosive devices at the Mulberry Bush or the Tavern.

At the first of the two Court of Appeal references the Crown strongly disputed the correctness of that approach. On the first reference the Court of Appeal thought that there was 'a wealth of evidence as to surrounding circumstances, including information from members of the public, neighbours and acquaintances which by undesigned coincidences'[7] greatly strengthened the case against

the appellants'. Even if Mr Justice Bridge was incorrect in his
assessment and evaluation of the circumstantial evidence, the admissions being the 'hard essence of the case', was it reasonable to
suppose that the jury did not rely on such circumstantial evidence
to sustain its verdict, at least in supplement to the admissions? The
quashing of the verdicts at the stage of the second reference to the
Court of Appeal, three years later, did not canvass the circumstantial evidence as such; the flawed admissions sufficed to result in a
reversal of the jury's verdict. The Court thought that 'if the confessions had been shown to be unreliable, the prosecution case would
probably have failed'. But would it? Without a reasoned decision
from the 1975 jury, the question is speculative, if not unanswer-
able. Even if the prosecution case would have failed, if reliance
were placed exclusively on the circumstantial evidence, that does
not preclude the student from coming to his or her conclusion. As
I indicated in the Prologue, I am to be counted among the agnos-
tics about the true perpetrators of the terrorist crime.

III

The Value of Circumstantial Evidence

Whenever a commentator on criminal justice talks of a prosecution depending on 'purely circumstantial evidence' (which is, to my mind, nowadays an all-too-frequent occurrence) I bristle with professional indignation. Is there any truth at all in the assumption that circumstantial (or, indirect, if you prefer) evidence is intrinsically an inferior brand of evidence? A moment's pause and thought about evidentiary material in a criminal trial is worth a volume of instantaneous assumptions about the quality of types of evidentiary facts.

The American author of the massive *Treatise on Evidence* (10 volumes, 1940 edition)[8] and of other books on evidence, Dean Wigmore, provides an authoritative starting point to the question posed.

There are two traditional ways in the Anglo-Saxon system of adversarial criminal proceedings of setting about to prove a case against an accused person. The first is to present to the court the thing itself as to which persuasion of the prosecution's case is desired. Instances of this method of procedure are the production of a bloodstained knife, the exhibit of an injured limb, the viewing of premises, or the production of a document. The second way is the presentation of some independent fact by inference from which persuasion is sought. This second way of proceeding to proof of a case falls further into two classes, the distinction between them depending on whether the basis of inference is the assertion by a human being as to the existence of the thing in issue, or inference to be drawn from any other fact. The former is termed 'testimony' or 'direct' evidence, couched in classical language by the academics as 'autoptic proference' (or 'eye-witness testimony'); the other inferential process is 'circumstantial' or 'indirect' evidence.

Apart from 'autoptic proference', all evidence involves an inference from some fact related to the proposition to be proved. The kinds of inferences fall naturally into two classes. Wigmore describes a simple special class of evidentiary facts separate from the mass, 'attended as it is with uniform and peculiar qualities affecting its probative features and long recognised in experience and acknowledged by jurists'. This special class of facts consists of the assertion of human beings used as the foundation of inference-drawing relative to the propositions asserted by them. This is known as 'testimonial evidence' or in practice, 'direct evidence'. All remaining facts form the class known as 'circumstantial evidence' or 'indirect evidence'.

James Fitzjames Stephen's draft of the Indian Evidence Act of 1872 was founded upon the distinction under two heads: (1) inferences from an assertion, whether oral or documentary, as to the truth of the matter asserted; (2) inferences from facts, which upon the strength of assertions do exist, or are believed to exist, to facts of which the existence has not been so asserted. The distinction thus expressed, by stating that all evidence is either direct or circumstantial, depends upon precisely the same theory. An American judge, Chief Justice Gilpin, put it neatly in 1873:

> As a matter of course, and from necessity, all judicial evidence must be either direct or circumstantial. When we speak of a fact as established by direct or positive evidence, we mean that it has been testified to by witnesses as having come under the cognisance of their senses, and of the truth of which there seems to be no reasonable doubt or question; and when we speak of a fact as established by circumstantial [or presumptive] evidence, we mean that the existence of it is fairly and reasonably to be inferred from other facts proved in the case.[9]

How, then, stands the relative probative value of the two classes of evidence? Wigmore provides a salutary warning against any conclusion that testimonial (direct) evidence is more persuasive than circumstantial (indirect) evidence. He states:

> The rules of admissibility have nothing to say concerning the weight of evidence when once admitted. The relative weight of circumstantial and testimonial evidence, therefore, does not present itself in this place. Indeed, it can be said that there are no rules, in our system of evidence, prescribing for the jury the precise effect of any general or special class of evidence. So far as logic and psychology assist us, their conclusions show that it is out of the question to make a general assertion ascribing greater weight to one class or the other; the probative effect of one or more pieces of either sort of evidence depends upon considerations too complex. Science can only point out that each class has its special dangers and its special advantages.

The question has been the subject of endless discussion. Judicial statements have often dealt with this question, rather more to eradicate *a priori* misconceptions than to declare any positive rule of law about the relative merits of circumstantial or testimonial evidence. But the pronouncements of the judiciary (few though they are) are not only instructive but are also deserving of prominent public display.

Judicial pronouncements are supportive of Wigmore's view that circumstantial evidence may be as persuasive and as compelling as testimonial evidence, 'and sometimes more so'. Innumerable decisions support the thesis that circumstantial evidence can provide a compelling demonstration of the existence or non-existence of a fact in the case. Wigmore drew particular attention to a classical judgment of Judge Furman in *Ex parte Jeffries* (1912)[10] and the former's editors noted that 'all laymen would profit by reading it'.

This is a case depending entirely upon what is known as 'circumstantial evidence'. It is therefore proper for us to consider the value of such evidence. Some courts hold that circumstantial evidence is of secondary importance and is inferior to what is called 'direct or positive evidence'. Our investigation and reflections have caused us to reach a different conclusion. All evidence is largely circumstantial, and even when most direct it depends upon circumstances for its credibility, weight, and effect. By way of illustration, suppose that a number of persons witness a homicide, and all testify that they saw A point a rifle at B, who was standing some 50 yards away; that they saw a flash and heard the report of an explosion; that they saw B fall to the ground, and upon going to his body found a small hole in his forehead and a similar hole in the back of his head; and that B immediately died. This would be called a case of direct and positive evidence. The evidence would be direct and positive only to the extent that they saw A point a rifle at B, that they saw a flash and heard the report of an explosion, that they saw B fall to the ground, that upon examination they found a hole through his head, and that he died immediately. No witness could testify as a matter of fact that he saw the bullet come out of the gun and pass through the head of B. That the witnesses saw a flash and heard the report of an explosion, based upon past experiences – that is, circumstances – would prove that A had fired the gun. Yet it would be possible that A may have missed B, and another may have fired the fatal shot. To carry this illustration further, suppose that half of the witnesses who saw the homicide testified that B was not attempting to make an assault on A at the time of this occurrence, and the other half of the witnesses testified that before A fired his gun B had fired at A. This would present an issue of fact to be settled by the jury, and the determination of this question would depend upon a great variety of circumstances, among which might be mentioned the interest or want of interest, bias or want of bias, of each witness in the case, the intelligence of the witnesses, the question as to whether or not they or any of them were suffering from any such physical or mental defect as would impair their sight, hearing, or memory, the viewpoint from which each witness saw the homicide, and the reputation of each witness for truth and veracity. Many other circumstances might be mentioned. All such circumstances must be considered by a jury in weighing the credibility of the witnesses in every case, whether it be of direct or circumstantial evidence. Suppose, for further illustration, we take the case of a contested will, where a number of witnesses testify that they were present and saw the testator execute the will and they signed the same as witnesses at his request, and their evidence is not disputed so far as human testimony is concerned; but, upon an examination of the paper on which the will was written, it is found that the date of the watermark in the paper was several years subsequent to the time of the death of the deceased, which would be the more satisfactory and therefore the best evidence, the direct testimony of these witnesses, or the circumstances of the date of the watermark in the paper? Suppose a number of witness testify that they saw a man thrust his hand into a bucket of water, and on taking it out a hole remained in the water where the man's hand had been. It matters not how positive and direct such testimony was, no sane jury would accept it. Why? Because their past experience, based upon circumstances, teaches them that it is contrary to the laws of nature for a hole to remain in water when a solid object is taken therefrom. This knowledge of the laws of nature and this past experience rest upon a great variety of circumstances too numerous to mention. A thousand different illustrations could be made to the same effect.

From these and other reflections we have come to the conclusion that it is a mistake to say that 'circumstantial evidence' is inferior to what is commonly called 'positive and direct testimony'. The truth is that no human testimony is superior to doubt even in cases of the most direct proof. It is always possible that witnesses may err unintentionally or may corruptly falsify their testimony for reasons which are at the time not apparent and not known. If the law required mathematical certainty either as to matters of fact or as to the conclusions drawn by the courts and juries, the enforcement of law would be impossible.[11]

If Wigmore's conclusion is derived almost exclusively from American sources, there is solid, if ancient, support to be found in the meagre English case law. In *The People* v *Tom Jones, alias Robinson* (1824),[12] Judge Smith Thompson in a New York case resurrected from obscurity Mr Justice Park's direction to the grand jury at Hertford Assizes, the previous year, in *R* v *Thurtell* as follows:

The eye of Omniscience can alone see the truth in all cases; circumstantial evidence is there out of the question; but clothed as we are with the infirmities of human nature, how are we to get at the truth without a concatenation of circumstances? Though in human judicature, imperfect as it must necessarily be, it sometimes happens, perhaps in the course of one hundred years, that in a few solitary instances, owing to the minute and curious circumstances which sometimes envelop human transactions, error has been committed from a reliance on circumstantial evidence; yet the species of evidence, in the opinion of all those who are most conversant with the administration of justice and most skilled in judicial proceedings, is much more satisfactory than the testimony of a single individual who swears he has seen a fact committed.

In *Annesley* v *Richard, Earl of Anglesea*,[13] summing up to the jury in a case of ejectment tried in Dublin, Lord Chief Baron Bowes said:

Mr Sergeant's reasoning ... was entirely agreeable to what I remember to have heard laid down by one of the greatest men who ever sat in a court of judicature [a reference to Lord Coke] viz. that circumstances were in many cases of greater force and more to be depended upon than the testimony of living witnesses.

Witnesses, gentlemen, may either be mistaken themselves, or wickedly intend to deceive others. God knows, we have seen too much of this in the present cause on both sides! But circumstances, gentlemen, and presumptions, naturally and necessarily arising out of a given fact, cannot lie. And gentlemen, it must be left to your consideration, whether in this case as presumptions [arising from the kidnapping, and the prosecution for murder] do not speak stronger than a thousand witnesses.

A graphic illustration of the compelling nature of indirect (or circumstantial) evidence was given by Mr Justice Maule in the course of the argument before the Court of Crown Cases Reserved[14] in *R* v *Burton* (1854):[15]

If a man go into the London Docks sober without means of getting drunk and comes out of one of the cellars very drunk wherein are a million gallons of wine, I think that would be reasonable evidence that he had stolen some of the wine in that cellar, though you could not prove that any wine was stolen, or any wine was missed. [The accused's conviction was upheld.]

In *R* v *Exall and Others* (1866)[16] Chief Baron Pollock, sitting as a trial judge at the Kingston Assizes in a case concerning the so-called doctrine of 'recent possession' of stolen goods as evidence that might tend to show guilt as a thief, burglar or receiver, said of circumstantial evidence more generally:

It has been said that circumstantial evidence is to be considered as a chain, and each piece of evidence as a link in the chain, but that is not so, for then, if any one link broke, the chain would fall. It is more like the case of a rope composed of several cords. One strand of the cord might be insufficient to sustain the weight, but three stranded together may be quite of sufficient strength.

Thus it may be in circumstantial evidence – there may be a combination of circumstances, no one of which would raise a reasonable conviction, or more than a mere suspicion; but the whole, taken together, may create a strong conclusion of guilt, that is, with as much certainty as human affairs can require or admit of.

In *R* v *Taylor, Weaver and Tyson* (1928)[17] the Court of Criminal Appeal (the Lord Chief Justice, Mr Justice Swift and Mr Justice Branson) said:

It has been said that the evidence against the appellants is circumstantial. So it is, but circumstantial evidence is very often the best. It is evidence of surrounding circumstances which by *undesigned coincidence* [a phrase used in the judgment in the first reference appeal of the Birmingham Six at page 17 of the transcript] is capable of proving a proposition with the accuracy of mathematics. It is no derogation of evidence to say that it is circumstantial.

The only modern re-statement of the law on circumstantial evidence in criminal cases[18] is found in *McGreevy* v *DPP*,[19] a case in the House of Lords, on appeal from the Court of Criminal Appeal of Northern Ireland. Lord Morris of Borth-y-Gest analysed the law relating to the duty of a judge when directing the jury in a murder case, where a body of circumstantial evidence (and no other) existed, pointing to the accused as the guilty party. Counsel for the defence argued that, in such a case, the judge should not merely tell the jury that they must be sure of the guilt of the accused. In addition, he contended, the jury should be told that not only must the circumstances be consistent with the accused having committed the crime but also that the facts proved were such as to be inconsistent with any other reasonable explanation.

After a full analysis of the history of any possible obligation upon a trial judge to give such a direction,[20] albeit a discussion restricted to murder cases and not referring to any of the authorities mentioned in this section of this book, Lord Morris said that there was no rule of law requiring such a direction to be given. He did not think that it was even necessary for the judge to distinguish between circumstantial and direct evidence when formulating a direction. As he said, '… how is the judge to know what evidence the jury accept? Without knowing this how can he decide whether a case depends entirely on circumstantial evidence?' What was required was a summary of the evidence and an emphasis upon the need for the jury to be clearly informed that it could only convict if it was sure of the guilt of the accused.

In addition to this criminal case there is an interesting civil decision in Scotland from early this century. In *Miller* v *Mackinnon*[21] the Court of Session addressed the issue of the quality of circumstantial evidence in a case brought under the fatality provisions of the Workmen's Compensation Act 1906. This was a form of no fault liability upon the employer (in reality, upon the insurers) where the dependants claiming compensation had to prove only that the death arose 'out of and in the course of employment'. The brief facts were that the deceased was seen in his bunk in the early morning when his ship was moored in a river. An hour later he had disappeared leaving his clothes by his bunk. Two days later his body, in his night-clothes, was found near the mooring. He was unable to swim. There was medical evidence that he had drowned but no evidence as to how this had occurred. It was accepted that he had not committed suicide, being 'of cheerful disposition'. The lower court inferred form the evidence that the most likely cause of the drowning was that he had come up on deck while it was still dark and had fallen overboard. (Shades of Robert Maxwell?) That sufficed to make the ship owner liable.

On appeal it was argued that the lower court had drawn an inference that was unjustified, that the deceased might equally have fallen from the quayside and that explanation would have broken the link with his employment. Lord Dunedin, the Lord President, said that the issue was essentially one of fact for the lower court but he went on to make some remarks about circumstantial evidence generally:

It is said by [the employer's] counsel ... that there is an affirmative proposition to be proved by the [dependants] and that ... is not satisfied by simply proving that the man was found dead, but that you must establish the proposition that his death was by accident ... out of and in the course of his employment. But I opine that the determination of that proposition must still depend upon evidence, and must depend upon whatever class of evidence is available. The truth is that, when the matter is closely considered, there is after all no real difference between the result that the tribunal arrives at whether it is based upon direct testimony or upon what is called circumstantial evidence. Certainty is incompatible with human fallibility. However clear the direct testimony of a witness may seem to be, it may always be wrong, because the witness may be stating what he knows to be not the truth or, if speaking the truth, he may be mistaken in his own judgment with regard to the matters which he is relating. No human being can discover anything from which he draws conclusions except through the medium of some one of his senses, and any one of these senses is liable occasionally to mistake. Accordingly, it is almost, you may say, an accident whether direct testimony or the inference drawn from circumstantial evidence is the more cogent. Where you have direct testimony in such circumstances that you feel absolutely sure that the witnesses are speaking the truth, and where also it seems so improbable as to be almost impossible that they have been deceived in their senses in comprehending the matters from which they have drawn their conclusion, that is as satisfactory testimony as can be got. But there may be many cases where what is called circumstantial evidence may lead to results so certain that it is quite as good as, if not better than, direct testimony. There is a well known passage in *King Henry VI* where Shakespeare makes Warwick illustrate with regard to the death of a heifer the class of circumstantial evidence which brings certainty to all minds.[22] Accordingly, it seems to me that here, where there is undoubtedly no direct testimony, there is nothing antecedently wrong in saying you may come to a certain inference although that inference is only based upon circumstantial evidence.

The Court held that the inference drawn by the lower court was not only reasonable on the facts as found but was one that all ordinary people would draw. The burden of proof is, of course, higher in a criminal case than in a civil one, but the observations about the weight of circumstantial evidence apply to both types of proceeding with equal force.

Even taking account of these cases it is a pity that no other modern statement of the law exists. A further judicial corrective to ill-informed statements from non-lawyers is much needed.

At this point it must be added that Wigmore was well aware that in many cases circumstantial evidence would ultimately become a proposition to be proved by direct evidence. For example, the finding of a blood-stained knife upon the accused after a clandestine killing is a circumstance from which an important inference might be drawn. Yet the fact that the knife was found on the accused must itself be proved by the direct intervention brought about by the necessary testimony of some person. Wigmore thought that the great mass of evidence in litigation would require two steps of inference before its worth, weight and strength could be evaluated. First, the inference is 'from the fact of an assertion to the matter asserted. Then the inference is from the matter asserted to another matter ... from the fact of the making of the assertion to the truth of the matter asserted.'

Wigmore's conclusion that circumstantial evidence may be as persuasive as direct testimony is now generally accepted. What must always be remembered is what fact or facts the evidence in question is being used to support and what inference is being drawn from such fact or facts. As it was put by the prosecution in the American case of *Commonwealth* v *Borden*:[23] 'When Robinson Crusoe saw that [footprint] he knew that a man had been there who was not himself. It was circumstantial evidence. It was nothing but circumstantial evidence. But it satisfied *him!*' (original emphasis).

The cogency of circumstantial evidence

The very question of what amount, type or degree of any evidence that will suffice to prove an allegation has long been difficult to express in short form of words. As Mr Justice Birch in *R* v *Madhub Chunder* (1874)[24] put it:

> Unlike admissibility, the weight of evidence cannot be determined by arbitrary rules, since it depends mainly on common sense, logic and experience. Each case presents its own peculiarities and in each common sense and shrewdness must be brought to bear upon the facts elicited. The weight of evidence depends on rules of common-sense.

Lord Blackburn said in *Lord Advocate* v *Blantyre* (1879):[25]

> Therefore, as regards one accused, if it is shown that the police lied at the trial, depending on the rest of the evidence and the circumstances of the case, those lies may cause the court of trial to acquit or the Court of Appeal to quash a conviction. But as regards another accused, notwithstanding that police officers lied as to certain matters in the course of

the trial, the court of trial and the Court of Appeal may be certain of his guilt from other evidence in the case. The lies by the police may not affect the conclusion based on the remainder of the evidence that the accused is guilty beyond a reasonable doubt, although the lies will leave the police officers who have told them open to criminal prosecution or disciplinary proceedings.

Both these obscure authorities were cited by Sir Brian Hutton, Lord Chief Justice of Northern Ireland (now Lord Hutton, a Law Lord) in *R* v *Hill (Paul)* (1996)[26] quoting from *R* v *Latimer*[27] an earlier judgment of the Court of Appeal in Northern Ireland.

It used to be assumed that no conviction for murder could be arrived at without the discovery of the body. But this is not so. In a New Zealand case in 1952 (*R* v *Horry*)[28] a newly married wife disappeared. Her body was never found. Her husband was strongly suspected of the murder. He did not confess, the evidence against him being strongly circumstantial and a web of deceit practised by him when questioned by the police. He was convicted. On appeal, the court approached the case on the basis of a 'moral certainty' that the appellant had committed the murder by reference to the totality of the circumstantial evidence. A leading criminologist in the Anglo-Saxon world, in commenting on this case,[29] pointed out that in such cases we rely on the good sense of juries to appreciate and apply complex notions of proof and evidential analysis; yet we know virtually nothing of the reasoning process applied in the jury room.

Standard of proof

There is no duty on a trial judge to tell a jury that, in addition to being satisfied of the guilt of an accused beyond reasonable doubt, he must give a special direction about circumstantial evidence. A special direction would entail telling the jurors that they must be satisfied that the circumstances were consistent with the accused having committed the crime but also that the facts proved were such as to be inconsistent with any reasonable conclusion. In *McGreevy*, as indicated above, the House of Lords held that it was sufficient for the trial judge to give the traditional direction on the standard of proof, whatever the nature of the evidence. This accords with the general thesis that direct and indirect evidence alike call for a scrutiny of the evidence with scrupulous care. While this remains the law, there is nowadays (as reflected in the suggested direction for the Judicial Studies Board of February 1997 reproduced on pp. 87-8 below) a tendency to elaborate on the standard of proof. Where the case against the accused depends wholly or substantially on circumstantial evidence, it will be necessary to consider whether the evidence reveals any other circumstances 'which are or may be of sufficient reliability and strength to weaken or destroy the prosecution case'. The uncertainty engendered by this qualification of the law relating to evidential proof is a product of the division of function in decision-making. Where the decision to convict or acquit resides in a judge alone, such considerations will appear in the reasoned judgment.

Assume a hypothetical case: a number of men of Irish origin and of known political sympathies with the Irish Republican movement, are seen together shortly after two explosive devices are planted in public houses – as part of a recent series of bombings in the area in one of which an associate blew himself up, and the men were on their way collectively for the purpose of attending his funeral – would that be reasonable evidence of their complicity in an act of terrorism, even though there was no direct evidence that they had planned the bombing or planted the bombs? Stripped of the two other components of the Crown's case – the confessions and the scientific evidence – does the indirect evidence on its own add up to a convincing case of the Birmingham Six's guilt? Or was Mr Justice Bridge right to tell the jury that the circumstantial evidence did not rise above the level of suspicion, 'even strong suspicion'? Were the six men part of the terrorist gang responsible for the series of bombings in the Birmingham area in 1974, including the three on 21 November? The bombs did not find their way to the public houses without human activity and movement. The Six were behaving on that day, to say the least, in a very odd fashion. On the face of it they were merely planning a train journey (on which one of them was not going to travel) from New Street Station in Birmingham – two minutes away from the site of the bombings – to Heysham to catch the ferry to Belfast. The plan was to catch the 6.55 p.m. train. It is the facts surrounding that journey which provide the core of the circumstantial evidence.

IV

Background

At 8.17 p.m. on 21 November 1974 a bomb exploded at the Mulberry Bush Public House in the Rotunda building in Birmingham. Two minutes later another bomb exploded in the Tavern in the Town in New Street, Birmingham, two minutes walk away from New Street Station. Twenty-one people were killed and 160 persons were severely injured. The bombs had been placed in the two public houses around 5.30 p.m., or shortly thereafter. A third bomb planted at Barclays Bank, Hagley Road, Birmingham, was found before it could explode. Indisputably, the two bombings were not isolated incidents; they formed part of a concerted terrorist campaign in the Midlands at that time. Ten or eleven bombs or explosive devices in a series had been used. Thereafter there was silence from any terrorist activity in or around Birmingham. They were manufactured by a gang, each bomb being characterised by the use of the like equipment – a 125 Ever Ready battery, a wood screw, a warning light and the use of one or more ordinary alarm clocks. The latter were a penchant among some of the six; conversations often displayed an abnormal interest in alarm clocks; interest in them verged on the obsessive. Alarm clocks had been offered for sale in the public houses of Birmingham. In addition, a sketch plan was found among the possessions belonging to John Walker (one of the six accused) of an alarm clock with one hand missing; expert evidence was called to demonstrate that the explosive devices were constructed out of an alarm clock with the hand missing.

The events of 21 November 1974 were the culmination of the two earlier attacks – Constitution Hill, Birmingham on 5/6

November 1974 and the Telephone Exchange, Coventry on 14 November 1974, the latter of which exploded prematurely and killed one member of the gang. James McDade, the unfortunate victim of self-destruction, had an accomplice at the scene where he was arrested. That accomplice, who was in custody at the time of the events of 21 November 1974, and McDade were accompanied by other members of the gang who had planted bombs on 5/6 November and one of whom had been engaged in the planted bombs on 14 November 1974.

The Six were all acquainted with McDade, to a greater or lesser degree. According to Chris Mullin, McDade when he first came to Birmingham in 1968, lodged with Hunter in Aston for nine months; they last saw each other in late September when they were working together. Power, who came to England in 1963, had been at the same school in Belfast as McDade. Callaghan and McIlkenny also knew him, although less well than Hill. The Six knew each other before 21 November. Walker was a close friend of Hunter and McIlkenny. He took over from Hunter in April the treasurership of the raffle competitions for the Prisoners Dependants' Fund. He gave the money to another member of the McDade group for transmission to Dublin. McIlkenny was also concerned in that organisation. Power used to drink in the Crossways with Hunter and Walker. Callaghan also knew Walker whom he would meet at the Crossways and Clubs. Hill knew Walker quite well.

On Wednesday 20 November the IRA issued a leaflet (a copy of which was found by the police among Walker's possessions). It read:

B. *Funeral Lieut. James McDade — died on active service 14.11.74*

The Irish Republican movement in England wish to state that on Thursday 21 November at 3.30 p.m. the remains of their comrade Lieutenant James McDade will be escorted from

Coventry mortuary to Birmingham airport and flown to Belfast. ...

We the Irish Republican movement consider that it is the duty of all Irish people in England to be present at Coventry mortuary, where a Roman Catholic priest will officiate ....

Support us in our struggle for which many have died.

The call was to be present in Coventry, not to attend any funeral in Belfast. At the trial, evidence was led to the effect that a message passed among Republican sympathisers that no one should go to the centre of Birmingham on the day of the funeral.

Before leaving his workplace on the day, Walker met a workmate, Tom Watt, in the locker room. Watt gave evidence at the trial that he had known that Walker was going to McDade's funeral because Walker had told him so the previous day. The conversation was significant only because Watt added that Walker warned him not to go out that night: 'I said, why? And he said, that's enough.' Watt claimed that was not an isolated remark. It was the latest in a series of such warnings given him by Walker. These warnings were each followed by explosions. Walker denied that he ever said anything of the sort; he even denied having met Watt on the day of the bombings. It was the same witness, Watt, who alleged that Walker had sketched out a diagram of a bomb, a crude sketch on the back of a cigarette packet. Watt also testified to a discussion about cheap clocks. (See Chris Mullin, *Error of Judgement*, pp. 23 and 184.)

Six minutes before the explosion at 8.11 p.m. on 21 November 1974, a warning of the presence of the bomb at the Rotunda and the public house near the tax office was given. The caller used a code which identified him as a member of the IRA. No warning of the bomb at Hagley Road was ever received. There was never any doubt cast on the view that all the bombings in November 1974 were the work of the same gang. McDade's death on 14 November inferentially would not deter his fellow terrorists from continuing to plant bombs. Association of the members of the gang could not add up to guilt, but it was a core circumstance.

McDade's remains were due to be flown back on the fateful day – 21 November – to Ireland for burial in Belfast, following a ceremony in Coventry. No such invitation was extended to be present at the funeral in Belfast. Yet five of the six men – excluding Callaghan – decided to be present at the funeral service in Belfast. During the day they, together with Callaghan, spent a great deal of time together. They gathered at Birmingham New Street Station from about 6.45 p.m. onwards. According to them, Power arrived first, followed by Hunter, McIlkenny and Walker and Callaghan who was not travelling. They were not waiting for Hill and intended to catch the 6.55 p.m. train which they said they just missed. In fact that train was late leaving New Street. It did not actually leave until 7.08 p.m. when, according to their account, they were all, save Hill, present at the station. Hill eventually arrived and joined them to catch the 7.55 p.m. train bound for Crewe. It mattered not that they caught the later train, since it would arrive in time for the ferry at Heysham, the only effect being a shorter wait at Crewe where they had to change trains.

During the critical period when the bombs were being put in position all six men spent a substantial time in the immediate vicinity. Their explanations for being in such close proximity to the targeted public houses at the crucial hour was that the four men who intended all along to catch the 6.55 p.m. train happened, for no discernible reason, to arrive late at the station and to miss it. Callaghan, who was not travelling, and whose wife was expecting him home to celebrate her birthday, decided to go to the station with them to have a drink. If they had caught the 6.55 p.m. train, however, there would have been no time (or very little time) for any drinking. Even if they did not arrive at the station in time to catch the 6.55 p.m. train, all five could in fact have caught it at 7.08 p.m. They were not, according to them, delayed because they were waiting for Hill.

Although the Republican call was for presence and support for

McDade in Coventry, each of those leaving by train from New Street Station intended to be present at McDade's funeral service in Northern Ireland. None of them had been back to Northern Ireland for some considerable time. When each of the five left his home in Birmingham for New Street Station, not one had warned any family or friend in Northern Ireland that he was travelling to Belfast. No one in Northern Ireland was expecting any of them. Hill and Hunter were both unemployed. Nevertheless they bought single tickets, when return tickets would have been cheaper, and Hill had borrowed enough money to pay for a return ticket. If Hill and Hunter bought single tickets only, it would appear to suggest that they intended to stay in Northern Ireland for an appreciable period, although their immediate families were living in Birmingham. Significantly, the tickets issued to Power, McIlkenny and Walker were issued sequentially; there could at least be no question of the three men travelling separately.

The cost of a ticket from Birmingham to Belfast return was £12.69. A single ticket cost £7.51. To purchase two singles was, therefore, considerably more expensive at £15.02. The two of them carried with them virtually no luggage. Given that their families resided in Birmingham, one wonders whether they were intending to stay away for a while, and if so why.

Money mattered. There was evidence that the Six were hard up financially. An associate's visit to Walker on 21 November was explained on the basis of an indebtedness of £1 only. Callaghan explained a similar visit on the same date to McIlkenny, also on the basis of a £1 debt. Power explained how he was accompanied by Hunter when he made a telephone call at New Street Station in order to repay him £2. So £3 mattered greatly, particularly perhaps to McDade's widow who might have appreciated contributions of £12.69 to the funeral expenses from each of them. After all, she was asking them to come to Coventry, not Belfast.

The suggested concerted move to be well away from the scene of the bombings and from any police swoop in the Birmingham area was thwarted by the alertness of the police in tracking down the five men at Heysham. Arrival in Northern Ireland at least would have put distance, in time and space, between the five men and investigating police officers.

On arrest, Hunter was not carrying *any* luggage at all. Walker, McIlkenny and Hill had baggage with them, although their possessions were minimal and very light. Power's personal possessions were placed in Walker's baggage. Yet when Walker left home to travel to the station, the sheer weight of his luggage attracted the attention of an independent witness. When Hunter left home he had already manufactured a false alibi with his wife to account for his movements during 21 November.

At New Street Station Hunter made two telephone calls. According to him, he also made a further call at Crewe station. He said that each call was made to Northern Ireland. For each he had an innocent explanation. He had made no calls to Northern Ireland before leaving his home and the defence witness who was supposed to have received all three calls asserted that he had received two, not three telephone calls from Hunter that evening. On his own evidence, therefore, one telephone call by Hunter was not accounted for. Was it the call just after 8.00 p.m. warning of the presence of the bombs at the two public houses?

At the time of arrest, none of the five travellers disclosed his intention to travel to McDade's funeral. Although the destination of each was the same, each spoke of a different destination to which arrival by families or friends in Northern Ireland was not expected. When initially interviewed hours later by the police at Morecambe Police Station, they each said they were on their way to McDade's funeral.

Callaghan did not travel with his five associates. It was his wife's birthday. He did not return home until 11.30 p.m. His god-daughter and her father described him as shocked and distressed. By the next day he knew that his five associates, who had been with him at New Street Station, had been arrested. Although he might have provided them with a cast-iron alibi, and although he visited Hunter's wife, he did nothing at all to help them.

There was, as I have indicated, abundant evidence of friendship with, and respect for, McDade by all six defendants, which persisted after they knew that he was a planter of bombs. Walker in evidence spoke of his bitterness at McDade's death. He thought it was a shame that McDade had blown himself up. Power regarded him as an object to treasure. Hunter, who had been Power's best man, was a very good and close friend of McDade. He admired his 'guts' when planting bombs. They saw each other frequently during the week after McDade's death. They spent the whole of 21 November toing and froing in each other's company, to each other's homes and other addresses. Apart from Hunter's false alibi about his movements that day, Hill was later to lie deliberately when he denied that he had seen Walker at 4 p.m. on 21 November. Between some of the six men and McDade there were very close links indeed. McDade was a bomb planter. Two other associates had been convicted of two separate bomb-planting conspiracies. According to one of those associates, he and others had attended the Bowdenstown celebrations in the summer of 1974 as 'representatives of the Birmingham IRA'! Among those who went with him were Hill and Hunter, plus the other associate.

During the previous summer, the Rotunda Building had been attacked. On that night Walker had returned home very late with two other men. It was the second such incident observed by his neighbours. On this occasion all three men carried into Walker's house large blue plastic bags from the boot of a car. During October and November Walker and McIlkenny had been preoccupied with alarm clocks. On a number of different occasions during this period they were seen in possession of, buying or arranging for the repair of numerous alarm clocks. The inference to be drawn from this significant evidence was underlined by two independent witnesses who had heard Walker describe features of the bombs which, in at least one case, showed a considerable similarity to the bombs manufactured by the gang in which McDade had been a member.

The most critical evidence linking Walker and McDade was the unchallenged fact (admitted by Walker at the trial) that in July 1974 he had been entrusted by McDade to take a bag or bags, which contained McDade's bomb-making equipment, to the home of another associate of McDade. That associate took the equipment (about 100 detonators) to another man. On 28 November, after his arrest, Walker voluntarily took the police to that latter man's home. If Walker did know that the bag contained bomb-making equipment which he had been harbouring, it was deadly evidence against him.

The issue of nightly delivery of bags arose out of the evidence of Mrs Wickett, a neighbour of Walker, about the delivery of the bags, late at night, to Walker's home. Chris Mullin in his final chapter, 'Aftermath' (p. 399) in his book *Error of Judgment*, aware of this powerful piece of evidence, tackled Walker with the evidence two months after the Birmingham Six were released in 1991. Walker is reported to have said: 'It was bricks and plaster: I was knocking it off from work. To build a fireplace at home.' Mullin asked: 'Who delivered it?' Answer: 'A workman on night shift. A Brummie, I can't remember his name. He had a car. I didn't have any transport.' Recognising that Walker had some explaining to do, Mullin asked pertinently why Walker did not say that at the time of his trial. The answer was: 'Too embarrassed. It was thieving, wasn't it?' Mullin obtained confirmatory evidence from Walker's daughter that her father had told her that the bricks were stolen. Mullin frankly observes: 'In the absence of the Brummie who delivered the building materials coming forward, there is, of course, no definitive proof that there is an explanation for Mrs Wickett's evidence.' Without this explanation, given years after the event, the jury at Lancaster Crown Court in 1975 might be forgiven for having drawn an adverse inference from a powerful piece of evidence implicating Walker in terrorist activity. And if the jurors had been given the explanation afforded to Chris Mullin, would they have accepted that anyone on a murder charge would not reveal a piece of minor thieving?

The police evidence

Strictly speaking, the conduct of the police is irrelevant to the nature of this short book. But since so much has been said about the physical violence which the Six experienced, the point needs to be made, for the record, that police 'brutality' formed no basis of the quashing of the convictions.

The five men who had travelled in company were arrested in Heysham, four of them at the barrier. Hill, who had gone ahead of his four co-travellers, was taken off the boat. All five were taken to Morecambe Police Station; they all said they were on their way to attend McDade's funeral. The next day – Friday 22 November – police from the West Midlands went to Morecambe where the Lancashire Police were holding the five men. Interviews were held; the five were taken back to Birmingham, where Callaghan was arrested. On Saturday 23 November all six were interviewed. On Sunday 24 November the six were photographed; only Walker's bruise under one eye was revealed.

While a plethora of evidential matter was directed, at inordinate length, to the issue of the reliability of the confessions, thus diverting the jury's attention from the circumstantial evidence, one fact was never in dispute. On the Monday morning of 25 November all six men were brought before the Birmingham justices in a crowded courtroom and were remanded in custody to Winson Green prison until 28 November. Except for a small mark on Walker's eye (which he told his solicitor had happened when he fell) no one in court that day noticed any sign of any mark of violence of any kind having been inflicted on any of the six accused. The doctor who examined the six men at the request of their solicitors on 26 November was not called to give evidence before the jury at their trial. The doctor's evidence had been given in the trial-within-a-trial. But their legal advisers elected not to put that evidence subsequently before the jury.

When all six men were returned to the Magistrates' Court on 28 November, the picture was very different. In the civil proceedings, five years later, brought against the two relevant police forces[30] the facts were related in Lord Denning's idiosyncratic style of judgment-writing:

> At their appearance there were gasps of astonishment. They [the six men] had been beaten up. Their faces were black and blue. The journalists reported it. The papers were full of it.

The appalling, unforgivable, physical violence to which the Six had undoubtedly been subjected, was conveniently retroflected by the defence so as to support allegations of protracted assaults during the weekend when the six men were in police custody at either or both Morecambe and Birmingham Police Stations, undergoing police interviews.[31]

This episode served to bolster the ability of the six men to pursue their allegations that their confessions had been rendered inadmissible on the grounds of improper extraction of them by force. The doctor's evidence in the 1976 trial of the prison officers was at no stage deployed by the defence during the reference to the Court of Appeal in 1987. It obviously did not assist the case for the six men. The case advanced by the Six of police brutality developed and changed, becoming ever more central to the theme as it advanced. The case put to the officers was of violence of a different magnitude to that eventually spoken of, which paled into insignificance compared with the allegations made in the civil proceedings. For example, an allegation by Hill in a television programme years after the event, about the holding of a lighted cigarette close to his eye, had never been mentioned previously in court.

V

Unsafe Verdict: An Unsatisfactory Approach

When the case of the Birmingham Six was referred for the second time to the Court of Appeal, the Crown did not seek to resist the appeal. But it engaged, unsuccessfully, in contending that while the jury's verdict should be set aside on the ground that it was 'unsatisfactory', it was not 'unsafe'. Lord Justice Lloyd, unfairly, dubbed the Crown's approach as an 'exercise in damage-limitation'. It is true that, since its introduction in the Criminal Appeal Act of 1966 (consolidated in 1968),[32] the dichotomy between 'unsafe' and 'unsatisfactory' had never been seriously canvassed as supplying a discrete challenge to a jury's verdict of guilt. Counsel for one of the two appellants in *Stafford and Luvaglio v Director of Public Prosecutions*[33] (a notorious killing in the north-east of England in 1972) did, in his reply before the House of Lords, point to the disjunctive wording, and added that 'it is possible to have a verdict which is safe, but nevertheless is unsatisfactory' (p. 888H). He did not apparently elaborate his submission, although earlier, in opening his appeal, he had used the word 'unsafe' on its own in relation to the court's function on receipt of fresh evidence (p. 885B). None of their Lordships made any direct allusions to the submission. Lord Kilbrandon, a Scots Law Lord, no doubt imbued with the innate provision in Scots criminal justice of an intermediate 'not proven' verdict, did, however, appear to appreciate the distinction. He said (p. 914B): 'I have come to the conclusion that the absence [of potential forensic evidence linking the appellants to the scene of the crime of murder] does not make the conviction, in all the circumstances, *unsafe* (italics supplied). The other Law Lords invariably deployed the composite language. In that case, of course, the verdict of the jury was challenged on the basis of the totality of evidence; hence the appellate courts could not have been concerned with holding that the verdict was unsatisfactory other than as a direct result of it being unsafe. Is the wording intrinsically productive of only a composite meaning; or does it lend itself to an interpretation of indicating two ways in which a conviction may be quashed, with the resulting label leading to different public responses?

The appeal of the Birmingham Six was in fact an appropriate case for arguing in favour of distinguishing the two distinct bases for setting aside a jury's verdict. In essence, the Crown conceded that the unreliability of the confessions and the flawed forensic evidence rendered the jury's verdict unsatisfactory. But it argued that there was left intact the residual, circumstantial evidence which could properly sustain the safety of the verdict. The Court of Appeal rejected the dichotomy of the phrase 'unsafe or unsatisfactory'. It said that the, admittedly disjunctive, words were a composite phrase indicating the interchangeability of the two words. Was the Court of Appeal right? Is it not possible for judges to arrive at a state of mind that concludes that the verdict is unsatisfactory, but is still safe? Such a conclusion might lead to a quashing of the conviction, but might not necessarily deny the possible complicity of the appellants in the criminal event. While the presumption of innocence at trial is properly to be preserved, there is room for not concluding that the successful appeal thereby renders the accused innocent. The English statutory provision defining the criteria for a successful appeal might be deliberately dichotomous to allow an appeal on one basis, but not on the other.

Broadly speaking (without reference to statutory construction and the jurisprudence on the criteria for allowing and dismissing appeals) the point can be put simply. If I have a spoke (or, perhaps, more than one) missing from my bicycle wheel, the vehicle is inferentially and objectively unsafe to ride. If I ride my bicycle in a wobbly fashion, my riding is unsatisfactory; it may or may not be unsafe either for myself or other road users. The test in that instance is, in part at least subjective. But what did Parliament intend by the two words, deployed disjunctively?

The legislative origins of the two words are to be found in the debates on the Criminal Appeal Bill of 1907. F.E. Smith, MP for Liverpool, Walton (later to be Attorney-General and Lord Chancellor as Lord Birkenhead) moved an amendment to the Bill on 29 July 1907 directing the Court of Criminal Appeal to allow an appeal 'if they think the verdict is, under all the circumstances of the case, unsafe or unsatisfactory'. This would have replaced the formula used in respect of a jury in a civil court – namely, allow an appeal 'on any ground on which the verdict of the jury might be set aside in a civil case' – a permissible range of appeal too narrowly circumscribed. In a civil case there had to be such overwhelming preponderance of evidence as to make a verdict so unreasonable as to be perverse – that is, such a verdict as no jury, properly instructed and assisted by the judge, could return. In opposing F.E. Smith's amendment, but undertaking to find an acceptable alternative, the Attorney-General, Sir John Walton, said:[34]

The rule which would be applied if the Bill stood as drawn would be this. If the Court of Appeal thought that reasonable men properly instructed could not have arrived at the verdict at which the jury had arrived then they might set it aside, but only then. His hon. and learned friend suggested the insertion of the words 'unsafe and [*sic*] unsatisfactory'. He did not know what meaning they should attach to the words. He believed that if they were inserted it would afterwards be held that 'unsafe' must be used in connection with some canon of safety, as, for instance, danger to public safety under the conditions in which the law was being administered. The words 'unsatisfactory' was equally open to doubt, because it might be said, he thought it would be said, that an unsatisfactory verdict meant a verdict to which the existing standard of the House of Lords was applied and which showed that the verdict did not conform to that standard. He was very anxious that the matter should not be left obscure, and if his hon. and learned friend was prepared to accept the clause as it then stood he would take care that in another place the matter should be considered fully, and if words which were more satisfactory could be framed they should be framed.'

Ultimately the Criminal Appeal Act 1907 empowered the court to allow an appeal on any question of law and on fact 'if they think that the verdict of the jury should be set aside on the ground that it is unreasonable or cannot be supported having regard to the evidence' – a species of unsafeness? – or 'there was a miscarriage of justice' – a species of unsatisfactoriness? Additionally an appeal could be allowed if there had been a wrong decision on any question of law. In Scotland, the English formula was adopted. The right of appeal since the Criminal Appeal (Scotland) Act 1926 includes 'any alleged miscarriage of justice in the proceedings in which he [the appellant] was convicted'. Despite the change in England, under the Criminal Appeal Act 1968, Scotland adhered to the formula of 'miscarriage of justice' in section 228, Criminal Procedure (Scotland) Act 1975 which became section 106, Criminal Procedure (Scotland) Act 1995, and has remained unaltered after the change in England in the Criminal Appeal Act 1995.[35]

The F.E. Smith formula crept extra-statutorily into favour during the post-war years, and was specifically recommended in December 1964 by the Interdepartmental Committee on the Court of Criminal Appeal.[36] Section 2(1)(b), Criminal Appeal Act 1968 provided that an appeal should be allowed if the court thinks that in either one of three situations: (a) 'the conviction [formerly 'verdict of the jury'] should be set aside on the ground that under all the circumstances of the case it is unsafe or unsatisfactory'; or (b) 'the judgment of the court of trial should be set aside on the ground of a wrong decision of any question of law'; or (c) 'there was a material irregularity in the course of the trial'.[37]

Re-trial

On quashing the conviction, the Court may order a substituted verdict, or order a re-trial. The factors in deciding whether to order a re-trial are (a) that the innocent person should be formally acquitted by a jury: (b) that a 'guilty' person should not escape justice due to a defect in the trial process.

The power to order a re-trial was little used in the immediate years after its introduction in its present form in 1968. The Runciman Commission found that its use had increased between then and the early 1990s, and recommended that more use should be made of the power. The Court is disinclined to order a retrial whenever there has been an appreciable lapse of time between conviction and the successful appeal.

Presumption of innocence

If the Court of Appeal does not order a substituted verdict or a re-trial, the quashing of the conviction operates as a direction to the chief clerk of the Crown Court to enter an acquittal. That piece of administrative machinery merely perfects the order of wrongful conviction. As Dr Pattenden rightly comments:[38] 'Acquittal by direction of the Court of Appeal should not be regarded as a finding of innocence.'

There is no question of any revival of the presumption of innocence, which persists only so long as the jury does not record a verdict of guilty. Once that happens, the contrary is proved; the presumption is displaced ('rebutted' in the lawyer's language). The reasons are plain. First, there is nothing in the legislation which authorises the Court of Appeal, in quashing a conviction, to say whether it thinks that the successful appellant is innocent. This was what the Court of Appeal said in the second reference appeal in 1991 when it talked of the 'task of deciding whether a man is guilty falls on the jury' as being 'a point of constitutional importance'.

A second reason is that in our criminal justice system it is not just those who are in fact truly innocent who are entitled to have their convictions quashed. Those, for example, who have been prejudiced by a want of due process (not having had a fair trial) are entitled to the same result. Sir Frederick Lawton, a distinguished Lord Justice of Appeal from 1972 to 1986 – he had been a High Court judge experienced in criminal trials since 1961 – has been quoted as having once remarked how 'extremely irritating' it is to see a person who has had his conviction quashed 'prancing in front of the television cameras saying: "I have been proved innocent" '.

There is a third reason, advanced by the purists among the legal profession. It is claimed that the jury has not even the power to declare someone innocent. Despite a common popular view to the contrary, a verdict of not guilty does not mean that the accused was not responsible for the crime; it means only that in law he must be treated as if he did not commit it. As Professor Zander, a member of the Runciman Commission, put it in an article in *The Times* in 1994:

> It is true that as a principle of our system there is a presumption of innocence. But that does not mean that an acquittal officially serves as a declaration of innocence. The presumption of innocence exists quite independently of whether the defendant is innocent or guilty, and indeed has nothing to do with the question of guilt or otherwise.

'Not Guilty' may often arouse the feeling of 'not proved', but the intermediate verdict of 'Not Proven' in Scottish criminal procedure has no counterpart in England. The effect of a 'Not Proven' verdict is the same as that of 'Not Guilty', in that the accused is released and cannot be tried again for that offence. The implication, however, is that he has escaped conviction only because of some slight (not wholly unreasonable) doubt or some technicality in the trial process. It is claimed by Scottish lawyers that the 'Not Proven' verdict is a valuable preventive against unjustified verdicts of Not Guilty.

The origins of the grounds for allowing criminal appeals

Before questioning the Court of Appeal's conclusions on the proper construction of section 2(1)(b) of the 1968 Act, it is necessary to complete the legislative history.

The three grounds for allowing an appeal – a wrong decision on any question of law, a material irregularity in the course of the trial, and a conviction which is unsafe or unsatisfactory – are replaced in the Criminal Appeal Act 1995 by a single ground that the Court of Appeal 'think that the conviction is unsafe'. This dropping of the disjunctive phrase, in favour of the single ground, followed the recommendations of the Runciman Commission which had been set up on the day of the quashing of the convictions of the Birmingham Six. The change in England did not find favour in Scotland. A report of the Independent Committee on Criminal Appeals and Miscarriages of Justice Procedures (the Sutherland Committee) to the Secretary of State for Scotland in June 1996 adhered to the 'miscarriage of justice' formula. It said:

> We do not believe that the case has been made by the proponents of change for abandoning the concept of 'miscarriage of justice' as the ground for an appeal. Nor do we believe that, if change were to be necessary, it would be acceptable to move to the formulation of a conviction being 'unsafe'. There is no body of Scottish jurisprudence which relates to the concept of an 'unsafe' verdict. It would be a novel concept in Scottish criminal law. By contrast the ground of 'miscarriage of justice' and the scope of the Appeal Court's powers in relation to the disposal of appeals have been in use for a considerable period of time and have been judicially considered and clarified in many cases in a way which shows them to be capable of adaptation and development to meet contemporary understandings of justice in criminal appeals. This approach is firmly rooted in the Scottish legal system and

offers suitable flexibility. We regard this as the best and most appropriate way forward in Scottish circumstances.

The genesis of the phrase 'unsafe or unsatisfactory' pre-dated its introduction in 1966. Apart from F.E. Smith's attempt in 1907 to persuade Parliament to anticipate the legislative provision of 60 years later, the Court of Criminal Appeal between 1907 and the late 1960s had used such extra-statutory language in performance of the statutory duty to allow or dismiss an appeal.[39] An indication of that judicial approach was elucidated recently in the High Court of Australia in *M* v *The Queen* (1994).[40] The test for applying section 6(1) of the Criminal Appeal Act 1912 (New South Wales) – a replicate of section 4(1) of the English Criminal Appeal Act 1907 is as follows: namely, the Court will allow an appeal if:

> of opinion that the verdict of the jury be set aside on the ground that it is unreasonable, or cannot be supported, having regard to the evidence, or that the judgment of the court of trial should be set aside on the ground of a wrong decision on any question of law, or that on any other ground whatsoever there was a miscarriage of justice.

The majority of the High Court of Australia said:

> Where a court of criminal appeal sets aside a verdict on the ground that it is unreasonable or cannot be supported having regard to the evidence, it frequently does so expressing its conclusion in terms of a verdict which is unsafe or unsatisfactory. Other terms may be used such as 'unjust or unsafe' or 'dangerous or unsafe'. In reaching such a conclusion, the court does not consider as a question of law whether there is evidence to support the verdict. Questions of law are separately dealt with by s 6(1). The question is one of fact which the court must decide by making its own independent assessment of the evidence and determining whether, not-

withstanding that there is evidence upon which a jury might convict 'nonetheless it would be dangerous in all the circumstances to allow the verdict of guilty to stand'. But a verdict may be unsafe or unsatisfactory for reasons which lie outside the formula requiring that it be not 'unreasonable' or incapable of being 'supported having regard to the evidence'. A verdict which is unsafe or unsatisfactory for any other reason must also constitute a miscarriage of justice requiring the verdict to be set aside. In speaking of the Criminal Appeal Act in *Hargan* v *R*,[41] Mr Justice Isaacs said:

> If [the appellant] can show a miscarriage of justice, that is sufficient. That is the greatest innovation made by the Act, and to lose sight of that is to miss the point of the legislative advance.

The High Court also said:

> The test [for allowing an appeal] ... is the discernment of a verdict that is unsafe or unsatisfactory. That does not call for the application of what has been called a 'speculative or intuitive basis' and does not extend to the English subjective test that an Appeal Court discern 'some lurking doubt in our minds which makes us wonder whether an injustice has been done'. The question, in Australia, is one of fact which the court decides, making its own independent assessment of the evidence: in doing so it assesses whether, on the whole of the evidence, it was open to the jury to be satisfied beyond reasonable doubt that the accused was guilty. The court will not allow itself to substitute trial by court of appeal for trial by jury, for the ultimate question must always go back to determining whether the jury could have been satisfied beyond reasonable doubt.

The pinpointing of 'miscarriage of justice', favoured by the Scots

lawyers, has never found universal favour in English judicial cir-
cles; hence its partial abandonment in 1966 and its final demise in
1995, with the removal of its negative form in the proviso to the
grounds for allowing an appeal. The essence of the problem lies in
the extent to which Parliament in 1966 was merely giving declara-
tory effect to the judicial language, or was deliberately giving
differential effect to the two disjunctive words.

At the hearing of the second reference to the Court of Appeal in
1991, Crown Counsel, Mr Graham Boal, sought to argue that
even if the convictions of the Birmingham Six were unsatisfactory
(which he was conceding they were) nevertheless they were not
necessarily unsafe. In the course of the argument, Lord Justice
Mustill asked him whether it was the gist of his submission that
Walker, in the light of the compelling evidence against him, independent of the police evidence or the scientific evidence alone,
would have been convicted 'and that he would have brought the
other defendants down with him?' The transcript records counsel's
laconic answer: 'Mr Boal: Yes. (Cries of dissent from the public
gallery).'

Chris Mullin's comment (*Error of Judgement*, p. 397) was:

> So there it was in a nutshell. Nothing had changed. No matter
> that the forensic evidence was worthless. No matter if the
> confessions were forgeries and if a large number of officers
> were lying. No matter that the convictions were about to be
> quashed. The Birmingham Six were guilty and that was that.
> To this day such comforting sentiments may be heard wher-
> ever two or three senior lawyers or police officers may be
> gathered.

The Court of Appeal was no less dismissive of Mr Boal's argument. In one page of a 74-page judgment which took $2\frac{1}{2}$ hours to
read the Court said:

> [Mr Boal] pointed out, correctly, that the words unsafe or

unsatisfactory are disjunctive. He referred us to a number of reported cases (there must be many more unreported cases) from which it appears that in allowing appeals the court sometimes uses one word, sometimes the other, and most frequently both together. It was said that we might discern a pattern. But if so we failed. Lord Devlin suggests a possible distinction at page 158 of his book [*The Judge*] assuming the words are not tautologous.[43] It has never been argued in any reported case that the words bear different meanings, save, in passing, by Mr Hazan QC in the course of his argument in reply in *Stafford and Luvaglio*. In *Graham* (1975)[44] the court contemplated that a conviction might be unsatisfactory without being unsafe; but the circumstances were very special. It has never been decided by any court that there is a difference in meaning,[45] and we could see no purpose in Mr Boal advancing the argument that there is such a difference in the present case.

Chris Mullin described Boal's argument as 'gobbledegook ... a good old fashioned smear', what Jeremy Bentham once coined as 'grimgribber nonsense'. The Court of Appeal did say in effect that the conviction could be safe and at the same time unsatisfactory – that is, 'to imply guilt while simultaneously conceding defeat'– without accepting any distinction between 'unsafe' and 'unsatisfactory'. It quashed the conviction on the grounds that it had been obtained unlawfully, but made it plain that it was not thereby inferring innocence. It said:[46]

Where we allow an appeal we are directed by section 2(2) to quash the conviction. Where we quash the conviction, the order operates, by virtue of section 2(3) as a direction to the trial court to enter a verdict of acquittal, except where a retrial is ordered under section 7 of the Act. Nothing in section 2 of the Act, or anywhere else obliges or entitles us to say whether we think that the appellant is innocent. This is a point of great constitutional importance. The task of deciding whether a man is guilty falls on the jury. We are concerned solely with the question whether the verdict of the jury can stand.

Surprisingly, since otherwise his book is admirably comprehensive in its coverage, Chris Mullin does not mention this crucial passage. Indeed, he makes no mention at all of the contents of the final judgment at the second appeal in 1991.

Other wrongful convictions

Often – rather too often – the ultimate result of the Birmingham Six case is linked with the quashing of other contemporaneous convictions, all being labelled, indiscriminately, as miscarriages of justice and the successful appellants 'innocent'. But in the case of the Guildford Four the revelation that the confessions had been obtained unlawfully undermined the Crown's case such that the convictions were rendered unsafe, as well as being unsatisfactory. Lord Lane pointedly observed, in delivering the judgment of the Court of Appeal (p. 11):

> From that necessarily brief précis of the way in which the case proceeded it will be seen that, in reality, everything depended upon whether the jury were satisfied so as to feel sure that the police evidence in relation to the various interviews, and consequently upon the statements which came afterwards, was to be relied upon or not.
>
> It follows that any evidence which casts a real doubt upon the reliability or veracity of the officers who were responsible for the various interrogations must mean that the whole foundation of the prosecution case disappears and that the convictions will in those circumstances be obviously unsafe.

and again at p. 15,

Those matters deal primarily with the cases of Armstrong on the one hand and Hill on the other. The cases against Conlon and Richardson are obviously intimately bound up with those events. We of course do not know what the jury would have made of the matter. Our task is to determine whether we think the convictions of Conlon and Richardson are made *unsafe* (italics supplied) by what we have heard. We have no doubt that the convictions of all of these four appellants in respect of the Guildford and the Woolwich events *unsafe* (italics supplied), even though the latest revelations have no direct bearing on the evidence relating to the Woolwich bombing.

On that footing the Guildford Four were, and are absolutely entitled to claim that the jury's verdict could not stand safely, whereas the Birmingham Six were wrongly convicted on the grounds of an unfair trial.

The Bridgewater Three

Four men – Vincent and Michael Hickey, James Robinson and Patrick Molloy – were charged with murder and aggravated burglary on 19 September 1978 at Yew Tree Farm, Woodsley in the West Midlands. The victim was a 13-year-old boy, Carl Bridgewater, who, while riding his bicycle on his newspaper round in the direction of the farm, was killed by a single cartridge from a shotgun. Patrick Molloy, who was then 51, was convicted of manslaughter and aggravated burglary. He was sentenced to twelve and eight years' imprisonment respectively and consecutively. The other three were convicted of both murder and aggravated burglary. They were sentenced to life imprisonment. Patrick Molloy died in prison in June 1981; his application for leave to appeal lapsed with his death. (Section 7 of the Criminal Appeal Act 1995 removes this procedural barrier.) In March 1987 the Home Secretary referred the cases of the three to the Court of Appeal; the appeals were dismissed in March 1989. On 29 July the Home Secretary again referred the convictions of all three to the Court of Appeal. These appeals were held during the Spring of 1997. They were successful, the three being released on unconditional bail at the outset of the hearing. Judgment was delivered on 31 July 1997.

Two reasons were advanced for referring the case to the Court of Appeal. First, it was not disclosed to the appellant's lawyers until December 1994 that unidentified fingerprints found at the scene of the crime included three usable prints taken from the boy's bicycle, one of which was Carl Bridgewater's and the other unmatched to any of the three appellants. Second, there was material that indicated the unreliability of a statement taken by the police from Patrick Molloy. That statement, confessing to his presence at the farm, was made only after Molloy had been shown a statement purporting to be that of Vincent Hickey. A supposed signature of Vincent Hickey was subjected to Electro-Static Document Analysis and found to be a forgery. Molloy's confession had thus been improperly obtained by the deceit of police officers – a case of a material irregularity. The prosecution conceded that Molloy's conviction could not be sustained, although it was not argued whether the contents of the statement were true or not. The Crown went on to say that there was no answer to the proposition that the three appellants had not, therefore, received a fair trial; the admission of Molloy's 'confession' infected the whole trial, a questionable conclusion, having regard to the authority of *Lord Advocate* v *Blantyre* (p. 38 above) The convictions of the three appellants were 'unsafe' and duly quashed. (Michael Hickey's appeal was quashed on the ground that a reasonable jury, properly directed, could not properly convict on the evidence.) The Court of Appeal, composed of Lord Justice Roch, Mr Justice Hidden and Mr Justice Mitchell, delivered a reasoned judgment of 397 pages (a summary of 12 pages was mercifully provided). The Court was quick to say that it was 'not going to carry out an inquiry as to whether the appellants were in fact innocent' because it was 'neither empowered ... nor armed with the necessary powers to do so'. Yet such disavowal of any determination of guilt or innocence was prefaced inexplicably by the sentence in the judgment:[47] 'If we concluded that the convictions were unsafe then the convictions would be quashed *and the presumption of innocence which exists in favour of all unconvicted persons would be re-established* '[48] (italics supplied). This is a highly questionable statement of the law. Indeed, it is probably wrong. The presumption of innocence survives only unless and until there is a conviction at the hands of the jury; the presumption is thus displaced. A subsequent quashing of the conviction does not resuscitate the presumption, since the appeal court is concerned only with ensuring the propriety of the trial process and the substantiation of the jury's verdict. The Court acknowledged the 'the guilt or innocence of the appellants is not relevant to this appeal in absolute terms but only with regard to the safety of their convictions'. The Court of Appeal's assertion of the 're-establishment' or 'reinstatement' of the presumption of innocence might be vouchsafed only if the single ground of a successful appeal since 1995 – 'unsafe' – was intended to have the effect of automatically erasing the jury's verdict to the point of revival of the presumption of innocence. No reasoning along these lines was offered. And I doubt that any valid reason could be advanced from the language used in the new statutory provision in the Criminal Appeal Act 1995.

'Unsafe or unsatisfactory': a question of statutory construction

It is noteworthy that the Court of Appeal, in the first reference in 1987, ended its judgment with the words: 'We have no doubt that these convictions were both safe *and* satisfactory' (italics supplied). By using the words conjunctively, the Court could not have been meaning to say that 'or' could be held or construed to mean 'and'. As Lord Reid said in *R* v *Federal Steam Navigation Co Ltd*,[49] it would be quite wrong for any court so to construe a disjunctive phrase conjunctively. Lord Reid went on to say that, nevertheless, there was another applicable principle of construction:

In very limited classes of circumstances, it has been held proper to strike out a word from a statute or other writing and to substitute one or more other words for the words struck out.

But there is no authority that I am aware of that displaces the primary task of giving every word used by the legislature some meaning. The Court may not simply pronounce that Parliament has indulged in a piece of supererogation by the use of two words meaning precisely the same, unless the words are manifestly interchangeable. 'Unsafe' is not linguistically the same as 'unsatisfactory'.

In the *Federal Steam Navigation* case, Lord Wilberforce began his judgment thus:

> My Lords, it is important to state precisely what we are asked to decide in this appeal. It is to determine the meaning of the following phrase – extracted from section 1(1) of the Oil in Navigable Waters Act 1955:
>
>> If any oil ... is discharged from a British Ship ... the owner or master of the ship shall, ... be guilty of an offence under this section.
>
> To say that what we have to decide is whether 'or' is conjunctive or disjunctive or, putting it more bluntly, whether 'or' means 'and', appears to me, with respect, to be a dangerous simplification. It is the meaning of the phrase as a whole that concerns us.

All the Law Lords in that case agreed that the courts had power to treat the section as though the relevant words were 'the owner and/or the master'. What divided the House was the question whether the concept of a criminal offence gave the Crown an unfettered discretion to select which of the two persons should be criminally liable. The result was to avoid such a legal monstrosity by applying 'surgery rather than therapeutics'. In logic, there was no rule that required that 'or' should carry an exclusive force.

By parity of reason, it would be a legal monstrosity to suggest that both concepts 'unsafe' and 'unsatisfactory' had to be satisfied before a conviction could be set aside or, as a matter of language, that they should be treated tautologously. Adopting Lord Wilber-force's approach, what is the meaning of the phrase in section 2(1) of the Criminal Appeal Act 1968 as a whole? The phrase is '… the Court of Appeal shall allow an appeal against conviction if they think – (a) that the conviction should be set aside on the ground that under all the circumstances of the case it is unsafe or unsatis-factory'.[50]

The first thing to note is that the statute is dealing exclusively with the appellate function of the criminal law; it does not disturb the 'diacritical variant' – the mark of distinguishing the different values of acquittal and conviction – of the trial verdict. Quite the contrary, it does not extinguish or nullify the verdict of guilt; it only sets it aside. The *New Shorter Oxford English Dictionary* (1993) gives as the primary meaning of 'set aside', 'discontinue the performance or practice of' or 'dismiss from consideration', and only secondar-ily, 'reject as of no value, cogency, or pertinence; overrule; discard or reject from use or service, in favour of another'. An alternative meaning given is '(chiefly Law) annul, quash, make void, vacate'.

If section 2(1)(a) was to be read as a whole, may it not have been Parliament's intention (as evinced by the true meaning of what they said)[51] to confer a power on the Court of Appeal to allow an appeal if it thought that the conviction should no longer have any practical effect for either one or other of two alternative reasons. Thus it would be left to the appeal court to distinguish between the unsound verdict of guilt based on the material adduced before the jury (and any other additional evidence) and the conviction which was arrived at by a failure in the application of due process without detracting from the content and substance of the evidential mate-rial?

Unsafe or unsatisfactory: which?

The proposal of the Royal Commission on Criminal Justice (the Runciman Commission) in 1993 was to replace the existing law by a general broad ground – whether the conviction 'is or may be unsafe'. The effect of that proposal was that convictions would in the future not be quashed where, despite an error of law or a material irregularity in the trial process or pre-trial malpractice by the police or prosecution, the conviction remained 'safe'. The Home Office in its discussion paper on the Runciman proposal endorsed the view that the Court of Appeal should be concerned only with the safety of the conviction and not with acting as a 'quasi-disciplinary body, "punishing" errors or incompetence in the trial process'. Safety (unqualified by a 'may be') of conviction became the sole criterion in the 1995 Act for allowing an appeal.

If there had to be a choice between the supposedly interchangeable words, 'unsatisfactory' rather than 'unsafe' would seem to be preferred, so as to reflect the Runciman Commission's otherwise expressed desire to encourage a greater willingness in the appellate system to interfere with jury verdicts. 'Unsatisfactory' is a good word, since it covers anything ranging from 'there is something fishy', alternatively, 'a lurking doubt' about this conviction, to a closely reasoned demolition job by defence counsel of the evidential material. If in effect one were to draw a circle containing all the things that are unsatisfactory in the arrival of a guilty verdict, 'unsafe' would certainly be inside this circle. 'Safe', or any equivalent words, would, however, have to be encompassed by a separate circle. The difficulty about the all-encompassing use of 'unsatisfactory' is that it would sound odd for prosecuting counsel to describe the jury's verdict as satisfactory, when the attack by the defence is directed to an evaluation of the evidence – 'my Lords, the evidence was in a satisfactory state for the jury to convict'. 'Unsatisfactory' is appropriate, however, when limited to a material irregularity in the trial process, which does not affect the quality of the evidence.[52]

Did Parliament in the Criminal Appeal Act 1995, in its per-
ceived resolution of the debate, in fact deliberately abandon the
dichotomy between 'unsafe' and 'unsatisfactory', and did it not
simply endorse the ruling of the Court of Appeal that the words
were interchangeable, and hence prefer to use one word instead of
two? After all, as I have indicated, an unsafe verdict is by definition
unsatisfactory, but not *vice versa*. What do we mean by safe – safe
from what? Safe from a humiliating appeal decision? Safe, as it
were, from the indignation and reproaches of the person convicted,
or from the criticism of academic lawyers, or of society in general?
Or do we express the sense of a verdict being *secure* or impregnable
against any critical analysis (forensic, in all senses, or academic or
armchair, logical or factual, or whatever)? We could do some
thesaurus-thumbing, looking for words which we might use infor-
mally, like *unassailable, water-tight, certain, well-founded, solid, reliable,
conclusive,* or perhaps best of all, *incontrovertible.*

An appellate court may properly say the conviction (or the
verdict of the jury) is 'unsafe', in that it is clear that the convicted
person, who was found guilty on the evidence adduced at trial,
should not have been convicted. Apart from the tricky cases where
fresh evidence is admitted by the Court of Appeal and the court
has to evaluate the totality of evidence (the evidence at trial, plus
the fresh evidence) the 'safe' conviction or verdict may nevertheless
be 'unsatisfactory', in the sense that there has been some procedural irregularity which renders the trial 'unfair'. The words
'unsafe' and 'unsatisfactory' are not linguistically interchangeable,
although both are ultimately Latin derivatives. The reason why
English lawyers have tended to treat the words tautologously is the
diacritical variant of English law – the black and white of guilt or
innocence. As Lord Gifford QC, counsel for Hunter in the second
reference appeal, neatly said: 'English law does not recognise two
categories of acquittal; nor should it recognise two categories of
successful appeal.' We do not, however, need to emulate Scots law,
and confuse the trial jury with an alternative verdict of 'not
proven'. Innocence until proved guilty is a healthy maxim for a

civilised society to adopt up to the moment of primarily establishing criminal responsibility at trial. To maintain innocence beyond the point where failure to sustain a conviction on appeal, which relates to some irregularity, is not an imperative. Irregularity in the trial process does not displace the integrity of proven complicity as a result of the jury's verdict on the evidence, particularly where the evidence was circumstantial and had not been displaced.[53]

Three members of the Runciman Commission, in dissenting from the majority of their colleagues, thought that it would be confusing to wrap up all the possible grounds of appeal in the one word 'unsafe'. They considered (chapter 10, p. 169, paragraph 34):

> ... that the grounds of appeal should be redrafted to take into account two separate categories of appeal, those claiming that the verdict had been arrived at through an erroneous view of the evidence by the jury ... and those alleging material irregularities or errors of law or procedures in or before the trial.

This sound reasoning went unheeded.

There was some discussion during the committee stage of the Criminal Appeal Bill 1995 of the exact meaning of the word 'unsafe'. The Home Office minister, Mr Nicholas Baker, stated that the compendious term was intended to consolidate the existing practice of the Court of Appeal, thus rejecting the notion that 'unsafe' and 'unsatisfactory' are different concepts.[54] He preferred to take up another test that may be found in decisions of the Court of Appeal, namely, that a 'lurking doubt'[55] exists as to whether the conviction may stand. While this may simply be another way of expressing the word 'unsafe', it does not appear in the previous or present legislation. Whenever a court puts a gloss on statutory criteria there is a danger of moving away from those words towards some other formula not intended by Parliament to be used. Time will tell how both the Criminal Cases Review Commission and the Court of Appeal interpret the word 'unsafe'.

In practice the Court of Appeal pre-1995 rarely invited argument as to the precise meaning of the two words; nor did it pay much attention to the structure of its statutory jurisdiction. In 1968 in *R* v *Cooper*[56] Lord Widgery, commenting on section 4 of the Criminal Appeal Act 1966, said that the judges had to form a subjective opinion on whether they had a 'lurking doubt' about the correctness of the verdict. He added that 'this is a reaction which may not be based strictly on the evidence as such; it is a reaction which can be produced by the general feel of the case as the court experiences it'. This was the first occasion on which the Court had the opportunity of commenting on the new formula of 'unsafe or unsatisfactory'. However, in *R* v *Wellington*[57] Lord Lane rejected this test as too subjective and spoke of a need for a 'reasoned and substantial unease' about the conviction in juxtaposition to assessing whether the conviction was 'safe *and* satisfactory' (italics supplied).[58]

The only reported case I have been able to find where a very definite distinction was drawn between 'unsafe' and 'unsatisfactory' is *R* v *Llewellyn*.[59] Lord Justice Roskill said, in that case, where the appeal was founded on an improper indication from the trial judge of the consequences of plea bargaining, that the decision would be quashed for unfairness on the basis '*not that it is unsafe but that it is unsatisfactory*'.[60] He emphasised that the appellant was very fortunate, given the evidence and the fair conduct of the remainder of the trial and the lack of any mitigation in the circumstances of the offence.

The Antipodean approach in *M* v *The Queen*[61] fulfils the function of the evaluation of evidential material so as to determine criminal responsibility. It does not touch on those matters that are not within the jury's function and go to due process which may render the trial unfair (or unsatisfactory). As Sir John Smith QC argued in an article in the *New Law Journal* in 1995,[62] an example of the procedural irregularity was demonstrable in the case of *R* v *Algar*[63]

– a pre-1968 Act case. The conviction in that case was quashed because the appellant's wife, who was an incompetent witness, had been improperly allowed to give evidence at the trial. The Lord Chief Justice, Lord Goddard, told the appellant that he had a lucky escape: 'Do not think we are doing this because we think that you are an innocent man. We do not. We think that you are a scoundrel'[64] – an unsatisfactory verdict, but certainly not unsafe! Now that under the 1995 Act the Court of Appeal has lost its power to apply the proviso ['notwithstanding the court might decide in favour of the appellant, it can dismiss the appeal if it considers that no miscarriage of justice has actually occurred'] it may have to confirm a conviction, however unsatisfactory the trial has been, so long as the procedural irregularity has not endangered the safety of the conviction. Mr Baker thought that the word 'unsafe' would cover procedural irregularities such as to make the verdict unacceptable.[65] That is unsatisfactory.

However, during the passage of the Bill through both Houses of Parliament, there was no questioning of the conclusive view of the Court of Appeal that the words 'unsafe' and 'unsatisfactory' were interchangeable. Indeed, one MP, Mr Oliver Heald, a practising barrister until he became a junior minister in 1995, went so far as to say that he knew nobody who could tell him the difference between an 'unsafe' and an 'unsatisfactory' conviction.[66] Only Lord McIntosh of Haringey, a non-lawyer, speaking for the Labour opposition, said that he did not agree that the words bore no difference in meaning but had to concede that 'for practical purposes, we agree that there is no distinction'.[67] The only debate on the proposed grounds for allowing an appeal was a minor departure from the recommendation of the Runciman Commission which had opted for the formula, 'unsafe or may be unsafe'. In moving the second reading of the Bill, the Home Secretary said:

> The Bill clarifies the grounds for allowing appeals on three overlapping grounds which is widely felt to cause confusion. Under the Bill, the Court of Appeal will allow any appeal

where it considers the conviction to be unsafe and will dismiss it in any other case. This simple test clarifies the terms of the existing practice of the Court of Appeal, and I am pleased to note that the Lord Chief Justice has already welcomed it.[68]

When the Bill went to the House of Lords, Lord Taylor, the Lord Chief Justice, did indeed support the Government's suggested change in the language for setting aside a jury's verdict, and added for good measure that there was no merit in including in the simple test the words 'or may be unsafe'. He considered that the implication of doubt was inherent in the single word 'unsafe'.

It is puzzling to note that nowhere was any mention made, if only of rejection, of the dissenting note of the three members of the Runciman Commission, including the relevant passage in Professor Zander's personal note of dissent. It may be that the innovative provisions setting up the Criminal Cases Review Commission so dominated the thoughts of parliamentarians that it sufficed, for once, to accept unquestioningly the view of Lord Justice Lloyd and his colleagues in the second reference appeal in the case of the Birmingham Six.[69] The criminal appellate system deserves a re-run of the Donovan Committee of thirty years ago. Or perhaps the system should form part of a more comprehensive review of criminal justice (see Blom-Cooper & McConville, *A Case for a Royal Commission on Criminal Justice and the Penal System*, Prison Reform Trust, December 1996.) The issue, nevertheless, is worthy of further debate and legislative consideration.[70]

A European dimension

In support of a distinction between the two words in the previous (1968) Act, one might conveniently point to the effect of the European Court of Human Rights' application of Article 6 of the Convention which guarantees a fair trial. Article 6(1) of the Convention provides as relevant:

> In the determination of ... any criminal charge against him,
> everyone is entitled to a fair hearing by an independent and
> impartial tribunal established by law.

Article 6(2) provides that 'everyone charged with a criminal offence
shall be presumed innocent until proved guilty according to law'.

In *Murray* v *United Kingdom*[71] the Court at Strasbourg (by 11 to 7
votes) held that authorised delay in a detained person's access to
legal advice for 48 hours, sanctioned by section 15(8) of the Northern Ireland (Emergency Provisions) Act 1987 [now section 45(7) of
the Northern Ireland Emergency Provisions Act 1996] was a
violation of Article 6(1) in conjunction with Article 6(3)(c). This
latter provision confers on the accused the right to legal assistance
in defending himself.

There was a violation, even though the effect of having been
denied access to his solicitor had had no adverse consequence on
the detained person, since he had, without the advice of the
solicitor, still chosen not to answer any questions put to him during
police interviews. The violation of the Convention did not, however, render the conviction invalid ('unsafe'), but it certainly did
comprehend an unfair ('unsatisfactory') trial. This is because a
violation of the Convention by a Government does not affect the
validity or invalidity of the verdict of the municipal court. Likewise
the result of the case of Ernest Saunders: *Saunders* v *United Kingdom*.[72]
The division of function between a violation of Article 6 of the
Convention and the appellate process in the municipal courts is
exemplified in *R* v *Morrissey*,[73] where Lord Bingham, the new Lord
Chief Justice, explained why a conviction was to be upheld although the European Court of Human Rights would declare that
the procedural irregularity rendered the trial unfair. In both cases
the complaint was that evidence had been admitted which incrimi-
nated the defendants in circumstances where it had been obtained
compulsorily in the course of a DTI investigation into the affairs of
limited companies. In the latter case Lord Bingham reasoned that
a breach of the Convention could not override a plain provision of

domestic law even if, under the Convention, the principle of a fair trial under Article 6 had been infringed. As and when the Convention is enacted as part of English law our judges will doubtless adopt the like approach to an Article 6 violation.

In *Saunders* the European Court added pointedly at the end of its judgment[74] that it [the court] 'cannot speculate as to the question whether the outcome of the trial would have been any different had use not been made of the transcripts by the prosecution [footnoting a reference to *Murray* v *United Kingdom*] and, like the Commission, underlines that the finding of a breach of the Convention is not to be taken to carry any implication as regards that question.' Accordingly the Court considered that a finding of a violation by itself constituted just satisfaction in respect of any non-pecuniary damage sustained (Mr Saunders had sought £1 million damages to compensate him for the denial of his right to a fair trial and the resulting anxiety, anguish and imprisonment) over and above the costs of the European proceedings. It would seem that English law is thus more generous than European human rights law. Whenever a conviction is quashed in England on the ground that the verdict was 'unsafe' or (as previous to 1995) 'unsatisfactory' as a result of an unfair trial, the successful appellants are entitled to be compensated for the periods of loss of their liberty irrespective of the reasons for concluding a wrongful conviction: see section 133, Criminal Justice Act 1988.

In *Leutscher* v *Netherlands*[75] the European Court of Human Rights distinguished a violation of Article 6 from the fact of a conviction by the Dutch court. The ruling, given on 26 March 1996 (a month after *Murray* and before *Saunders*), established that an appellate court in a country was – both under the European convention and under domestic law – entitled to take into account the suspicion which still weighed against the individual as a result of the fact that his conviction had been quashed on appeal only because the prosecution was found to have been time-barred when the case was brought to trial. The Court made clear that nothing in the documentation of the case in the Dutch proceedings or in the case at

Strasbourg gave any cause to doubt the correctness of the conviction. Thus a material irregularity may violate Article 6. It does not thereby disturb the propriety (safety) of the conviction.

Recently, in *Coyne* v *United Kingdom*[76] the Court (of nine judges including the UK member) held unanimously (following earlier jurisprudence) that the system of Courts-Martial in England was not sufficiently impartial and independent to meet the requirements of Article 6 of the Convention. The Court did not award compensation for pecuniary losses, i.e. income and earning capacity, since the date of the conviction. The Court was not prepared to speculate as to what the result of a fair trial might have been. Indeed, the accused conceded that he had not been *wrongly* (as opposed to *unfairly*) convicted (emphasis added). He merely contended that he had not had a fair trial. The Court said (para. 60) that:

> the applicant did not contend that he was wrongly convicted or sentenced, or that the Court-Martial would have reached a different verdict had it been organised in accordance with the Convention.

The Criminal Cases Review Commission

If Parliament in the Criminal Appeal Act 1995 has foreclosed on the Court of Appeal formally distinguishing between the two ways in which a conviction is quashed, there is an opportunity for injecting some juristic sanity into the appellate process, at least in the reference cases. That opportunity is provided in the other innovation of the 1995 Act, the Criminal Cases Review Commission.

The Commission is an independent body with powers to investigate complaints of miscarriages of justice and, where appropriate, to refer them back to the Court of Appeal. It replaces the role of C3 division of the Home Office.

It has at present fourteen members of whom at least a third must be legally qualified under the statute. In practice about a half are so qualified. The chairman is in fact a non-lawyer. It can direct investigations by the police in the area in question or it may carry out its own investigations. The criteria for making a reference to the Court of Appeal are that:

(a) there exists an argument or evidence which gives rise to a 'real possibility' that, in the event of a reference, the conviction will not be upheld;

(b) that the argument or evidence has not been previously raised before a court;

(c) or that other exceptional circumstances exist which justify a reference back to the court.'

The powers of the Commission

When it makes a reference, the Commission must provide a statement of its reasons for doing so.[77] If it refuses to refer it must also
provide a statement of reasons.[78] The phrase might suggest that a
summary of the Commission's reasons will suffice in both instances.[79] But that is an unlikely interpretation. As stated above, the
powers of the Court have been changed so it must consider the sole
question, whether the conviction is 'unsafe'. Given the duty to give
reasons, the Commission will have to identify what it thinks is
potentially wrong about the conviction, differentiating between
procedural irregularities and substantive merit. In turn, the Court
will in every case have to say why the conviction is or is not unsafe.
In doing so, it will have to grapple with the problems discussed
above[80] about the meaning of the word. So far there is no guidance
from the Court, but since judicial review is applicable the Commission may one day be told by the High Court the full extent of its
powers and duties. The High Court is likely to say that the duty of
the Commission is to give no more extensive a statement of its
reasons than would be the case should a similar requirement be
imposed upon a minister or administrative body. After all, the
Commission is not a judicial body and, therefore, does not have to
give reasons of the nature and quality a judge would have to
provide.

In *R* v *Stock*[81] the Court of Appeal dealt with a case referred by
the Home Secretary under his now-repealed powers. Fresh evidence was made available to the Home Office in 1981, but it
refused to make a reference. Such refusal was not challenged by
judicial review. Without giving reasons for its change of mind, the
Home Office did make a reference in 1993 adding no new material
to that which was available in 1981. The Court said that the Home
Office should, in the letter of reference, have given its reasons for
changing its mind. The Court added that it hoped that the Commission would do likewise, should it decide to refer a case which it

had previously decided not to refer. Such an obligation would seem to be inherent under section 14 of the Act.

The first reference to the Court of Appeal on 3 July 1997 in the case of Daniel McNamee gives no hint of the Commission's approach to its function under section 14, and no public pronouncement has so far evinced the Commission's intentions to declare its criteria for making or refusing a reference in relation to the power of the Court of Appeal to interfere with a jury's verdict.

A second reference was made on 22 September 1997 in the case of Mahmood Mattan who was hanged for murder in 1954! This is likely to be the first appeal to be heard under the new reference system. A third case involves two of the three men convicted of the M25 murders.

The Commission seems to have got off to a good start.

VII

Conclusions

It is not just the passage of time which has dimmed the evaluation of the evidence laid out before the jury in the case of the Birmingham Six. The judicial definitiveness about the propriety of the Birmingham Six's convictions was pounced upon by the supporters of the six men who, abetted by the media, succeeded in their incessant public efforts, not only ultimately to have the convictions set aside but in the process to undermine public confidence in English criminal justice. The former activity was laudable: the latter, opportunistic and misguided. The activists were rightly intent in their campaign, which was directed to demonstrating that the verdict of the jury was 'unsatisfactory', on the grounds that the forensic evidence was flawed and the confessions improperly obtained. But this campaign could not primarily be directed at showing that the verdicts were 'unsafe'. In pursuing their campaign, however, they focused persistently on the first reference to the court – judgment in 1988 – and personally attacked the members of the court and by inference, the institution itself.

This skilful attack has been sustained by public acceptance of the view that 'miscarriages of justice' had undermined confidence in the criminal justice system. Credence for that view was even accorded recognition in the address by Lord Woolf on the occasion of the thanksgiving for the life and work of Lord Taylor of Gosforth on 15 July 1997. Lord Woolf alluded to Lord Taylor's chief justiceship from 1992 to 1996 as having done, in Lord Woolf's view, much to restore public confidence in criminal justice after some 'regrettable miscarriages of justice'.

Each of the six men has been offered an award of compensation for his unjustified imprisonment, so far as money can ever adequately compensate for loss of liberty. The publicised offers of substantial awards may or may not seem adequate compensation for sixteen years in prison as a result of a wrongful conviction. (Any compensation is payable irrespective of the reasons for the quashing of the verdict.[82]) The amounts are calculated independently of Government by Sir David Calcutt QC. But, while as a society we must accept loyally, warts and all, the results of the judicial process, we should not instinctively disable ourselves from conducting a constant search and evaluation of the evidence alleged by the Crown as pointing to the six men's implication in the dastardly deed of killing and maiming innocent people. Might the circumstantial evidence, stripped of the embellishments and distractions of protracted proceedings, point to their complicity (perhaps with others unknown or unidentified) in a wicked crime? Would it be correct to say that the circumstantial evidence, elevated beyond the status of strong suspicion or conjecture, was sufficient to convict? Did the jury bring in a verdict that was controvertible? Had moreover, the jury not been absolved of the duty to return any verdict on the charge of conspiracy, it might have returned verdicts on the lesser charge which required only evidence of an attempt to cause explosions. Such questions abound. Answers depend on individual judgment. Agnosticism is perhaps the *only* safe answer. It is not the only conceivable answer.

The trial judge told the jury that the circumstantial evidence amounted only to suspicion (even highly suspicious behaviour), although when sentencing the six men he considered the verdict based 'on the clearest and most overwhelming evidence'. Since the exclusive decision-makers were the jurors, a single judge's view was no more than that, his opinion – an important one, nevertheless. The Court of Appeal in 1988 surely was not to be faulted, after an exhaustive scrutiny of the evidence, in expressing confidence in the correctness of the jury's verdict. *At that stage* its judgment could not be affected by the unreliability of the confessions or flawed by inadequate forensic material; the Court was simply recognising the jury's pre-eminence in decision-making. There was nothing to displace the judgment of the decision makers – twelve ordinary people who listened to the evidence and were satisfied so that they were sure (or, to use the well-worn formula, 'beyond reasonable doubt') that the six men were guilty.

The classical approach of the appellate court was stated by Lord Goddard, Lord Chief Justice, in *R* v *McGrath*:[83]

> Where there is evidence on which a jury can act, and there has been a proper direction to the jury, this Court cannot substitute itself for the jury and re-try the case. That is not our function. If we took any other attitude we would strike at the very heart of trial by jury.

The jury's verdict is still inviolable, unless and until its findings are demonstrably controvertible ('unsafe') or the trial process has been rendered irregular and unfair ('unsatisfactory') – assuming that this distinction is recognised in some manner or form after the 1995 Act. Will the Court of Appeal now, in quashing a conviction as being unsafe, nevertheless explain that the 'unsafe' verdict may have resulted from an unfair trial? Or will it shelter under the single rubric of safety, muddling the two aspects of jury trial? Clearly, the Court of Appeal in the Bridgwater Three case missed an opportunity of throwing some light on the obfuscation of the legislature.

Jury trial

According to D.W. Broeder,[84] two factors are claimed to induce trust in trial by jury. The first is that the 'community is said to have more confidence in the judgment of laymen than of those learned in the law'. The second is that 'complex and sometimes insoluble factual disputes have the appearance of being settled with ease when wrapped in the silent garb of a verdict returned in supposed compliance with strict legal rules'. But, as Norval Morris points out,[85] we know almost nothing of what thought processes go on in the jury room. At present we are denied by statute the possibility of learning about or researching into juries.[86]

Criminal justice, in its laudable aim to infuse the system with all the safeguards of due process,[87] simply went astray in the case of the Birmingham Six. In its fumbling attempts to achieve a just result, the appellate system misapplied the test of 'unsafe or unsatisfactory'. Linguistically, the words have different meanings, to which the courts should have given legal effect. The Court of Appeal should have quashed the convictions on the ground that they were unsatisfactory, leaving the question of 'safety' in the safe hands of *well-informed* public opinion.

Lord Devlin once wrote that 'the sleep of the final verdict is disturbed by the nightmare of miscarriage'. So it should be, but we should not allow the verdict of the jury – the sole determiners of fact – to be awakened from its peaceful slumbers by anything that is simply called by the name of miscarriage of justice (or a carriage of misjustice, as one commentator observed). Nightmares should be sparingly experienced, only when the moral conscience is properly aroused. Perhaps the discombobulation which is felt about some of the verdicts of our criminal courts – perverse acquittals as well as wrongful convictions – can be appropriately allayed and suitably corrected on appeal, only as and when decision-makers are called upon to articulate fully the reasons for their decisions.[88] Insistence on reasoned verdicts would lead to the demise of trial by jury. No twelve good men and women could compose proper, adequate and intelligent reasons this side of Doomsday. Imagine the jury at Lancaster Crown Court in 1975 having to compose a reasoned verdict of guilt on the Birmingham Six. It is a daunting thought, not to be contemplated by the proponents of trial by jury, let alone by a rational society. But so long as we cling to the fundamental right to jury trial for all serious offences, and endow the jury with the exclusive power to determine guilt or not, we must not be too assiduous in calling its verdicts into question. The danger is that, if no restraint is exercised, we will seriously undermine public confidence in the criminal justice system even more so than has the conduct of the police officers who were proved ultimately to have fabricated several of the confessions in the Birmingham Six and other cases.

The Interdepartmental Committee on Jury Service in 1965[89] stated that it was vitally important that the system of trial by jury should be 'fair, sensible and workable' for 'ensuring law and order are maintained, that justice is done and that liberties are to be preserved'. It concluded, however, that it did not wish to prejudice any future inquiry into the merits of the jury system, 'as to which we realise that there is room for divergent views'. Has the time come for that 'future inquiry' and for airing 'the divergent views'?

Dicey wrote in his *Law of the Constitution* (9th edition, 1945, p. 394):

> A distinguished French thinker [unidentified] may be right in holding that the habit of submitting difficult problems of fact to the decision of twelve men of not more than average education and intelligence will in the near future be considered an absurdity as patent as ordeal by battle.

Dicey added his own view that trial by jury was sustainable only so long as public confidence (or perhaps blind faith) resided in the system. If the view of the French 'thinker' is somewhat extreme, the idea that the guilt or innocence of an accused person can be appropriately determined by the say-so of the twelve ordinary citizens, without giving any reasons for their verdict (and no accountability for a perverse acquittal) may soon come to be regarded as either unsafe or unsatisfactory, such as to undermine public confidence that we operate in Britain a civilised system of criminal justice. Furthermore, it is no longer true that a plaintiff in a libel action has a right to insist on trial by a jury. As Lord Bingham of Cornhill sensibly pointed out in the case which Jonathan Aitken brought against the *Guardian* newspaper (where he was denied trial by jury), in a case of complicated facts there is a real need for a reasoned judgement of a trial judge and not merely a monosyllabic verdict from a jury.

The families and friends of all of the twenty-one people who died and the 162 injured on the night of 21 November 1974, together with those concerned about the effectiveness of the criminal process in bringing the Birmingham bombers to justice, might echo the words of a Chilean writer:

Although the truth cannot really dispense justice, it does put an end to many a continued injustice. It does not bring the dead back to life but it brings them out from silence.

Appendix

Circumstantial Evidence

The following direction is intended to cater for the type of case in which there is no direct evidence, but the prosecution's case is a complicated one made up of a number of pieces of evidence. In some simple and straightforward cases, no direction at all is necessary. In others the entire direction need not be given. However, in cases of difficulty or where e.g. much has been made in argument of the fact that the case is only circumstantial' it may be sensible to give the full direction. In *R* v *Stephens and Clarke* December 1995 95/1785/S2, Lord Justice Henry said (approving the direction below) that 'cases of difficulty cry out for a careful direction'.

Reference has been made to the type of evidence which you have received in this case. Sometimes a jury is asked to find some fact proved by *direct* evidence. For example, if there is reliable evidence from a witness who actually saw a defendant commit a crime; if there is a video recording of the incident which plainly demonstrates his guilt; or if there is reliable evidence of the defendant himself having admitted it, these would all be good examples of direct evidence against him.

On the other hand it is often the case that direct evidence of a crime is not available, and the prosecution relies on *circumstantial* evidence to prove guilt. That simply means that the prosecution is relying upon evidence of various circumstances relating to the crime and the defendant which they say when taken together will lead to the sure conclusion that it was the defendant who committed the crime.

[It is not necessary for the evidence to provide an answer to all the questions raised in a case. You may think it would be an unusual case indeed in which a jury can say 'We now know everything there is to know about this case'. But the evidence must lead you to the sure conclusion that the charge which the defendant faces is proved against him.]

Circumstantial evidence can be powerful evidence, but it is important that you examine it with care, and consider whether the evidence upon which the prosecution relies in proof of its case is reliable and whether it does prove guilt. Furthermore, before convicting on circumstantial evidence you should consider whether it reveals any other circumstances which are or may be of sufficient reliability and strength to weaken or destroy the prosecution case.

Finally, you should be careful to distinguish between arriving at conclusions based on reliable circumstantial evidence, and mere speculation. Speculating in a case amounts to no more than guessing, or making up theories without good evidence to support them, and neither the prosecution, the defence nor you should do that.

Notes

1. The appeals, on reference by the Home Secretary under section 17 (1)(a), Criminal Appeal Act 1968, were dismissed by the Court of Appeal (Lord Lane CJ, Sir Stephen Brown P and O'Connor LJ) on 28 January 1988. On a second reference the Court of Appeal (Lloyd, Mustill and Farquharson LJJ) allowed the appeals on 27 March 1991.

2. Clarendon Press, 1996, p. 369. Dr Pattenden slightly misquoted the passage, using the word 'case' for 'hearing', which might suggest that Lord Lane was commenting on matters beyond the appeal.

3. The six men were: Hugh Daniel Callaghan, Patrick Joseph Hill, Robert Gerard Hunter, Noel Richard McIlkenny, William Power and John Francis Walker.

4. The most persuasive advocacy asserting the innocence of the Birmingham Six is a book written by Chris Mullin, the Labour MP for Sunderland South and a freelance journalist. It is entitled *Error of Judgment: The Truth about the Birmingham Bombings*. It was first published in 1986, with a revised edition appearing in 1997. Mr Mullin has recently been appointed to be the chairman of the House of Commons Select Committee for Home Affairs.

5. The House of Lords has recently reviewed the law on the respective powers of the courts and the Home Secretary in cases of life imprisonment for murder: see transcripts in cases of *Pierson* [24 July 1997] and *Thompson* and *Venables* [12 June 1997].

6. P.4D, transcript CA.

7. See identical language in *R* v *Taylor* (1928) 21 Cr. App. Rep. 20, 21 and see p. 34 below.

8. This treatise was described by Associate Justice Blackmun in the Supreme Court of the United States as 'a renowned and accepted authority': see his dissent in *Coy* v *Iowa* 487 US 1012, 1029 n.3 (1988).

9. *State* v *Carter* 1 Houston Crim. Cas. 402, 410-11.

10. 7 Okla. Crim. 544.

11. A quotable phrase, if only for its succinctness, comes from *Miller* v *Cotton* 5 Ga 341, 349 (1848): 'Some circumstantial evidence is very strong, as when you find a trout in the milk.'

12. 2 Wheelers Crim. Cas. 451.

13. (1743) 17 Howell's State Trials 1139, 1405.

14. The Court was composed of Jervis CJ, Maule, Wightman and Williams JJ, and Platt B.

15. 1 Dearsley and PCC 282: 169 ER 728.

16. 4 F. & F. 922, 176 ER 850.

17. 21 Cr. App. Rep. 20, 21.

18. Some attempt at a direction to trial judges is derived from the recommended direction to juries on circumstantial evidence which is reproduced as an appendix to this book.

19. [1973] 1 WLR 276.

20. Referring notably to *R* v *Hodge* (1838) 2 Lew CC 227.

21. [1909] S.C. 373, 378.

22.   Who finds the heifer dead and bleeding fresh,

And fast sees bye a butcher with an axe,

But will suspect 'twas he that made the slaughter?

(Part II, Act III, Sc 2)

23. (27 AM L Rev 1893).

24. 21 WR Cr. 13, 19 (Ind).

25. 4 App. Cas. 770, 792.

26. Not yet reported.

27. Unreported.

28. [1952] NZLR 111.

29. Norval Morris (1952) 68 LQR 391.

30. *McIlkenny* v *Chief Constable of the West Midlands* [1980] QB 283 (CA); see [1980] 1 WLR for petition allowed and [1982] AC529 for outcome (*sub nom Hunter* v *Chief Constable of the West Midlands*).

31. The six men were assisted, in their otherwise unsubstantiated allegations, by statements made by prison officers at Winson Green prison during the inquiry conducted on 29 November 1974 by the Governor of the prison. (A subsequent inquiry was conducted by a senior officer of the Lincolnshire Constabulary; its conclusions were not revealed to the courts.) Those statements inclined to show that, whether or not prison officers had beaten the six men up, the police had done so before the six men were remanded in prison custody. At the trial in 1976 of 14 prison officers, a forensic doctor gave evidence adverse to the police. He concluded that the six men had been injured *before* the photographs had been taken on 24 November, but that they had also been injured while in the custody of the prison officers *after* the photographs were taken. All fourteen prison officers were acquitted.

32. See note 35 below.

33. [1974] AC 879.

34. Hansard HC Cols 632, 636, 29 July 1907.

35. It may be noted that as late as 1895 the judges were very much opposed to any appeal in criminal cases tried by juries other than on sentence alone or after reference by the Home Secretary. Their reason was that '... wide rights of appeal would tend to lessen the sense of responsibility of juries and are not required in the interests of justice'. See a letter from Lord Russell of Killowen for the judges to Sir Henry James: 30 LJ 333. Were the English judges, pre-1907, perspicacious in predicting that appeals against conviction by juries would not serve the interests of criminal justice?

36. 1965 Cd. 2755: Chairman Lord Donovan.

37. It is more correct to say that the change from the 1907 Act formula was made in 1966, since the later (1968) Act merely re-enacted a provision made in the former. The year is unimportant; the change did not appear conspicuously in the text of either the 1966 or the 1968 Acts. It had to wait for its effect until it was revealed by the House of Lords in *Stafford & Luvaglio* (see note 31 above).

38. *Op. cit.* p. 179.

39. The Donovan Committee pointed out that if there was a defect in the legislation then extant, it lay in the statutory language rather than in its interpretation by the Court: see para. 141, p. 32.

40. 69 ALJR 83.

41. (1919) 27 CLR 13.

42. at (1991) Cr.App.Rep. 274, 313.

43. Lord Justice James (a distinguished appeal court judge until his untimely death) regarded the introduction in 1966 of 'unsafe' and 'unsatisfactory' verdicts as different conceptually: see *The British Jury System*, papers presented to the Cropwood Conference in Cambridge, December 1974, p. 64.

44. 61 Cr.App.Rep. 292.

45. But see the case referred to in note 57 below which was not mentioned by the court.

46. (1991) Cr.App.Rep. 274, 313.

47. pp. 7-8 and also at page 85 at D.

48. The 12-page summary uses the word 'reinstated' (p. 7).

49. [1974] 1 WLR 505, at 508G.

50. In section 4(1) of the 1907 Act, it was the 'jury's verdict' and not the conviction that could be set aside. It was changed in order to allow for an appeal where the appellant had pleaded guilty.

51. In *Black-Clawson Industrial Ltd.* v *Papierwerke Wahldorf-Aschaffenburg AG* [1975] AC 591, 613 Lord Reid said: 'We often say that we are looking for the intention of Parliament, but that is not quite accurate. We are seeking the meaning of the words Parliament used. We are seeking not what Parliament meant but the meaning of what they said.' The intention to be attributed is determined objectively.

52. Research for the Runciman Commission carried out by Kate Malleson showed that 60% of successful appeals were based on errors by the trial judge: see *Review of the Appeal Process*, table 1.1. See also the note of dissent by Professor Zander, p. 233, para. 62, note 56.

53. See also 'Miscarriages of Justice and the Court of Appeal' [1993] 109 LQR 66 (R.J. Buxton QC, now Buxton LJ.) He believes that the two words were used interchangeably not because there is an intellectually compelling reason for doing so but because an argument addressed to a court that the two words had different meanings had no purpose. He pointed out that this must be so since the Court could allow an appeal on either ground. There clearly was such a purpose as Mr Boal's argument demonstrates. And see 'Criminal Appeals and the Criminal

Cases Review Commission', (1995) 145 NLJ 533 (Sir John Smith QC) and p. 72 below.

54. Hansard, Standing Committee B 21 March 1995, cols 25-28.

55. See p. 72 below.

56. (1968) 53 Cr. App. Rep. 82, 86.

57. [1991] Crim LR 543.

58. In *M* v *The Queen* (pp. 58-61 above) the High Court of Australia sided with Lord Lane, not Lord Widgery.

59. (1977) 67 Cr.App.Rep. 149, 156/7. The case was not cited to the Court of Appeal in 1991 in the Birmingham Six second reference on appeal.

60. In *R* v *Yorkshire HA, ex parte Baker* [1996], *The Times* 6 May 1996, I analysed the meaning of the words 'necessary or desirable' in a judicial review relating to rural pharmaceutical services. Relying on the *Federal Steam Navigation* case, I concluded that, in their legislative context, the two words could not be construed disjunctively.

61. See n. 20 above.

62. See n. 14 above.

63. [1954] 1 QB 27.

64. Reminiscent of that sentiment are the words of a famous nineteenth-century judge in Limerick. Discharging a prisoner, he is reported to have said: 'You have been acquitted by a Limerick jury and you may leave the dock without any other stain on your character.'

65. See Hansard cited at n. 54 above, col 27.

66. Hansard HC, Vol 256, Col 49, 6 March 1995.

67. Hansard, HL, Vol 564, Col 1492, 15 May 1995.

68. Hansard, HC, Vol 256, Col 24, 6 March 1995.

69. See p. 61 above.

70. One is reminded of the aphorism of Associate Justice Scalia in the United States Supreme Court: 'It is our task ... not to enter the minds of members of Congress – who need have nothing in mind in order for their votes to be both lawful and effective.' *Pennsylvania* v *Union Gas Company* 491 US 134 (1989).

For a more academic approach to criminal appeals generally in recent literature see Schiff and Nobles, 'Criminal Appeal Act 1995: The Semantics of Jurisdiction' (1996) 59 MLR 573; Nobles and Schiff, 'Miscarriages of Justice: A Systems Approach' (1995) 58 MLR 299; Nobles, Schiff and Shaldon, 'The Inevitability of Crisis in Criminal Appeals' (1993) 21 International Journal of the Sociology of Law.

71. (1996) 22 EHRR 29.

72. (1996) Cr.App.Rep. 1.

73. *The Times* 1 May 1997.

74. (1996) 22 EHRR 313, 342, para 86.

75. (1997) 24 EHRR 181, 194(31).

76. Judgment, 24 September 1997, transcript available on Internet.

77. s. 14 (3).

78. s. 14 (4).

79. However, the Minister, Mr Nicholas Baker, said in Committee (Hansard,

HC, Vol 258, Col 263)] that it was intended that full reasons should be given when the Commission refused to refer a case to the Court of Appeal.

80. pp. 66-74 above.

81. CA, 15 July 1996, unreported.

82. There are two schemes. One was created by s. 133 of the Criminal Justice Act 1988 and deals with appeals allowed because of newly discovered facts. The other is extra statutory and *ex gratia*. It deals with official misconduct leading to a wrongful conviction quashed on appeal or pardoned. There may be some overlap between the two schemes. See also s. 28 of the Criminal Appeal Act 1995.

83. [1949] 2 All ER at 497.

84. See his article 'The Functions of the Jury' (1954) 21 Chicago Law Review 386, 417.

85. See n. 10 above.

86. S. 8 Contempt of Court Act 1981. The present Government appears to be contemplating the removal of the ban on jury research: *Guardian* 13 October 1997, p. 9.

87. One is forcibly reminded of Mr Justice Cardozo's dictum, that 'justice, though due to the accused, is due to the accuser also'. To the like effect Lord Scarman said in *R* v *Sang* [1980] AC 402, 456E: 'For the conviction of the guilty is in the public interest, as is the acquittal of the innocent. In a just society both are needed.'

88. Such is the experience of judges in 'scheduled offences' trials without a jury in Northern Ireland: see Jackson and Doran, *Judge without Jury: Diplock Trials in the Adversary System*, Clarendon Press, 1995. In one of the 'supergrass' appeals, Lord Lowry CJ commented, 'experience in N.I. has shown how much greater in a Diplock trial are the appellant's opportunities of persuading the Court to interfere than when the appeal is from the sphinx-like verdict of a properly directed jury, which does not have to give reasons for its verdict': *R* v *Donnelly* [1986] 4 N.I.J.B.70.

89. Cmnd. 2627: Chairman Lord Morris of Borth-y-Gest.

Index

References to page and note numbers of this volume are given in bold type.